GORDON RAMSAY'S
PASSION FOR FLAVOUR

Gordon Ramsay's

GORDON RAMSAY'S PASSION FOR FLAVOUR

Text in association with Roz Denny
Foreword by Guy Savoy
Photography by Geoff Lung

Bounty Books

To my special mum Helen.
Thank you.

First published in Great Britain in 1996 by
Conran Octopus, a part of Octopus Publishing
Group Ltd

Reprinted in 1997, 1998, 200, 2001, 2004

This edition published in 2007 by Bounty Books,
a division of Octopus Publishing Group Ltd
2–4 Heron Quays, London E14 4JP

An Hachette Livre UK Company

ISBN: 978-0-753715-78-9

A CIP catalogue record for this book is available
from the British Library

Printed and bound in China

Editorial Director: Suzannah Gough

Project Editors: Katie Bell, Charlotte Colman-Smith

Copy Editor: Alexandra Carlier

Art Director: Helen Lewis

Designer: Peter Butler

Production: Jill Beed

Index: Hilary Bird

Contents

Foreword

Gordon Ramsay is a chef with passion, so it was inevitable that we would get along. From the first day he arrived in my kitchen I was enthralled by his vivacity and personality. We soon built a rapport – an understanding which has spawned unexpected results: for example, I taught him to hold a knife, now he asks me to pick up a pen!

Gordon is a chef in tune with his time. He both understands and uses principles that stem from modern cuisine but has added more than a sprinkling of his own talent. He is revered by his contemporaries for his gift with taste and flavour and has a faithful following, which I believe is the most flattering reward for any cook.

A great chef does not have to create heavy dishes to emphasize flavours. I am delighted his book reflects much of what he achieved during his time with me at rue Troyon. Gordon's attention to detail is exemplary: for example, in the strawberry garnish for his Crème Brûlée with Roasted Rhubarb, he uses a wonderful method of drying the fruit which makes it crispy and accentuates the taste. It is small discoveries like these which can make an unremarkable dish outstanding and, in turn, a competent cook a genius.

Introduction

I was not brought up with a food background. I did not pod beans at my grandmother's knee, gather forest mushrooms nor chase farmyard hens. My ambition was to play football for Glasgow Rangers which I set out to do in my late teens.

But I *was* born with an overriding desire to strive for perfection, to be the best in my field and to continue to move onwards and upwards. Football did not fulfil that side of my ambitious nature and, as a temporary distraction, I found myself in catering. A brief work-experience in banqueting, producing food for up to three hundred at one sitting did not satisfy my wanderlust either; but when I walked through the doors of a small, intensely personal kitchen in south-west London where the quality of food reigned supreme, I knew I had found my ultimate calling. I felt a growing sense of confidence in my abilities.

My two years working for Marco Pierre White at Harvey's marked the start of my formative years as a cook. I felt a great sense of freedom. Here was a field where I could express myself, where I could have a completely open mind and where I could excel. The more I learnt, the more I wanted to find out. Marco missed nothing; his personal touch was everywhere. No food was allowed to leave his kitchen until it had gained his approval. It was a style I admired and wished to learn from.

I went on to Le Gavroche in Mayfair, a larger kitchen with a more cosmopolitan brigade. The stay was fruitful, but my obsession for perfection made me look to France; and I knew I had to experience work there at first hand. Few English cooks went to work in France at that time. I was the only one in Guy Savoy's kitchen; and I then went on to work with Joël Robuchon – completely immersed in the culture and work environment. It was the only way to learn, and I soaked it all up, witnessing directly the depth of French enthusiasm and love of good food.

The French grow up with an innate respect for good food. A Frenchman buys bread twice a day, the English, twice a week. French butchers slice meat in front of you. Food buying is so personal. As I marched around the Bastille Market, picking cèpes, or prodding turbot, I developed an understanding for the French respect for and depth of knowledge about food. To me it was phenomenal. The repertoire of the French is far greater than ours and continues to grow.

I moved on to the kitchens of Guy Savoy where I spent many months at the side of the talented young pastry chef, Philippe Chapon. It was another great learning curve: I realized that good taste and perfection transcend boundaries and my quest for perfection could be satisfied in the pure art forms that were shaped on those dessert plates.

At the Aubergine restaurant we have come a long way in a short time. Our first Michelin star was given within twelve months of opening, followed by awards for Best Restaurant of the Year, Best New Chef and so on. But what gives me greater satisfaction is being fully booked a month ahead. That speaks louder accolades than awards. I am well aware that a chef is only as good as his last meal. Guy Savoy's parting advice to me was to be a star in my own kitchen and nowhere else. It is advice that rings true.

I have grown up quickly. Chance has given me opportunities few other young cooks have encountered. This growth has given me confidence; and I feel my creativity escalating, evolving and becoming more refined. If I had to categorize the important aspects of my style, I would place flavour way up in front. Flavour that comes from skill and techniques, not 'magic' or artificial ingredients. Nothing comes into my kitchen that has not been rigorously inspected by me or by my senior chefs. It has to be the best, my suppliers know that. The depth of flavour in our food stems from careful buying. The flavour in our sauces is achieved by reductions, skimming and yet more reductions – but not to the point of being heavy or cloying. The individual flavours must remain separate and light.

Freddie

Angela

Mark

Dominique

I like to give my clients value, but a value of quality not quantity. I do not wish them to consume three courses and retire to bed unable to move. I try to restrict the numbers at a table in the restaurant – no more than six people at a time, so that control of quality is maintained.

I feel that my bedrock will always be my small kitchen with its well-trained and enthusiastic staff who share and strive for the same ideals, totally immersed in producing food of the ultimate perfection. It is somewhat daunting to realize that when they place their careers in my hands they are also putting their lives on hold. Given the extreme hours we work in the restaurant kitchen, this shows great determination and strength of character, and I am grateful for that trust.

USING THIS BOOK

I do assume that those who buy this book to try the recipes have the skill of an enthusiast. It is not a book for the novice cook. Rather it is intended for those who find cooking a pleasure and wish to improve on their skills and share my ideas.

Most of the recipes are composed of a number of elements, mirroring the way we cook in the restaurant kitchen; so do read the recipes carefully in advance, and get your own *mise en place* ready. For example, do you need stock before making the Velouté, or the Confit for the garnish? The basic elements are easy to prepare in advance then store in the refrigerator. As all my dishes are put together freshly just before serving to maximize on the flavour, I suggest you do the same, tasting at every stage.

You may also find it helpful to read the Glossary (page 188), so as to become familiar with some of the terms we use in the restaurant kitchen.

Ian

Thierry

Jean-Claude

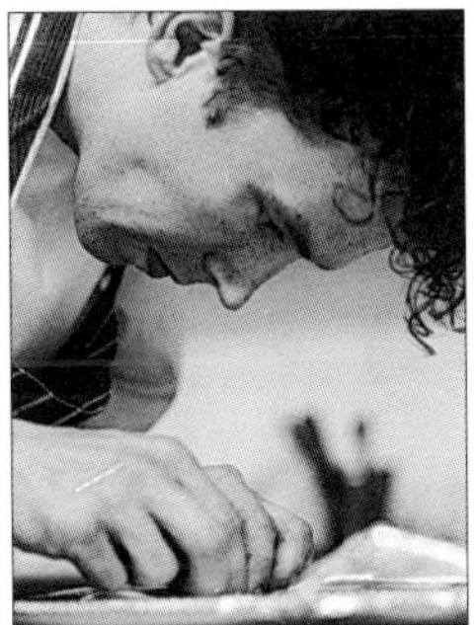

Damien

For example, we use the term 'roast' to mean exposure to intense heat on top of the stove, to brown and caramelize meat, fish or other foods.

At the back of the book, you will find a list of suppliers for certain foods and specialist equipment. I would suggest you track down top-quality butchers, fishmongers and greengrocers and establish a rapport with them. They might be more willing to stock the less common ingredients if they know you will be using them. Remember, the start of the chain of fine flavour starts with your suppliers and your ingredients.

MEASUREMENTS

I cook in metric in my kitchen, and, if you wish to ensure the measuring is the same, I recommend you follow suit. Most scales produced in the last two decades are in dual measurements, and most suppliers are familiar with the system. In addition, most food sold nowadays is in metric so it makes sense not to try to convert back to the old system. However, for those of you still using Imperial, I have given workable equivalents. Some equivalents, you will note, differ in their conversions according to the recipe. This is to keep proportions correct or to make them more user-friendly. For example, sometimes I use 3oz as an equivalent for 75g, sometimes 85g and sometimes 90g.

Building blocks

The most important time in our kitchen is from 7 until 11.30 a.m. It is time for mise en place *when much of our work is done. Thorough, careful preparation and good organization are ninety per cent of presenting an excellent meal. No matter what the dish, if the essential foundation preparation is not carried out correctly, then what follows is a waste of time. There is no time for corrections later.*

Many of my dishes are a combination of essential elements, or 'Building Blocks' as I prefer to call them. Obviously, I have a number of staff whose sole responsibility it is to supply me with these elements; but most of them can be prepared ahead by one person in a domestic kitchen, then chilled or occasionally frozen, ready for assembling at the point of finishing and serving.

I won't pretend that they are all quick and easy. There are few short cuts to ultimate flavour, but if the steps given are followed thoroughly and logically, then it is quite simple to achieve excellent results. Most of the Building Blocks given here are used in a number of my recipes, and many provide useful basics to have to hand when you want to allow your own culinary creativity to flow freely.

Stocks and sauces

For sheer depth of flavour, there is simply no real substitute for fresh, homemade stock when it comes to making sauces. The rich flavour of stock depends on fresh ingredients, the specific preparation of a foundation for flavour – the roasting of bones and the sweating of vegetables, followed by the long, slow simmering to draw out the natural bouquet of the ingredients; and, finally, the boiling down to reduce and concentrate flavour. Reductions are very important in stocks and sauces. In all my recipes, you will find directions to reduce down by a half or two-thirds – even with a stock that has already been reduced. This is what gives a sauce its depth, its intensity of flavour and, as no other 'magic' ingredients are needed, this keeps it light in texture too, neither cloying nor thick nor forming a skin.

The skill in making good stocks and sauces lies in patience: even an absolute beginner can make stock. If you can chop vegetables and regulate a cooker tap, you can make a good stock-base or sauce. All my stocks are made in the same way. They may take time, but they are undemanding and, at home, it's well worth making up a full batch and freezing it in 500ml/18fl oz/2 cup and 100ml/3$\frac{1}{2}$fl oz/$\frac{1}{2}$ cup blocks. That way, you'll always have your own 'stock-cubes' to hand, ready to produce sublime sauces.

1 A large pan, preferably a stockpot, of at least 12 litre/20 pint capacity is essential. If you don't have a stockpot then a preserving pan will do.
2 For brown stocks, it is necessary to roast the bones or carcasses initially in a very hot oven, turning occasionally. This gives flavour and colour to the stock. Any fat should be drained off before adding the bones to the stockpot. Light stocks and fish stocks don't require this initial browning.
3 As the stock comes to the boil, a scum will form. This is a natural accumulation of proteins and vegetable starches that will cloud the stock unless removed. Frequent skimming with a large, unslotted spoon is essential.
4 Do not season stocks with salt. There is enough natural salt in the vegetables, and as the liquor becomes reduced down, these will concentrate. Seasoning is generally added right at the end of the sauce-making process.
5 Finally, when the stock is ready, strain through a colander lined with a wet muslin cloth. Alternatively, an old, clean tea towel will suffice. When the stock cools, chill it and scrape off any fat that forms on the top.

Vegetable nage

A DELICIOUSLY LIGHT, NEUTRAL BASE FOR MANY OF MY SAUCES AND SOUPS THAT IS QUICK AND EASY TO MAKE, AND IDEAL FOR GENERAL USE. IN SOME OF MY SAUCES, I USE VEGETABLE NAGE IN COMBINATION WITH OTHER STOCKS TO LIGHTEN THEM. FOR MAXIMUM FLAVOUR, DON'T STRAIN OUT THE VEGETABLES AFTER COOKING. LEAVE THEM TO STEEP IN THE STOCK, THEN DRAIN SOME 24 HOURS LATER.

INGREDIENTS (makes 1.5 litres/ 2¾ pints/6½ cups)

3 onions, coarsely chopped
1 leek, coarsely chopped
2 celery sticks, coarsely chopped
6 carrots, coarsely chopped
1 whole head garlic, split in half
1 lemon, cut into 6 wedges
¼ teaspoon white peppercorns
¼ teaspoon pink peppercorns
½ bay leaf
4 star anise
2 litres/3½ pints/9 cups cold water
1 sprig each of tarragon, basil, coriander, thyme, parsley and chervil
200ml/7fl oz/⅞ cup dry white wine

1

2

1 Place the prepared vegetables along with the lemon wedges, peppercorns, bay leaf and star anise in a stockpot or large saucepan.

2 Add the water and bring to the boil, then adjust the heat to maintain a simmer for about 10 minutes.

3–4 Remove the stock from the heat. Add the fresh herbs and white wine. Push the herbs down into the liquid so that everything is submerged, then set the stock aside to cool and allow the herbs to infuse the stock with their flavourings.

3

4

5

5 When the stock is cool, pour it into jars and transfer it to the refrigerator. Continue the steeping process for about 24 hours.

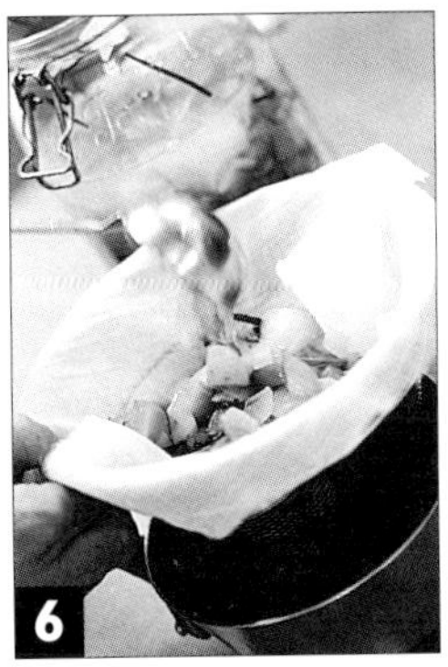
6

6 Strain the stock by pouring it through a muslin-lined colander set over a large bowl. Discard the vegetables, herbs and spices. The stock is now ready to use. Alternatively, chill or freeze it until required.

STORAGE

VEGETABLE NAGE WILL KEEP FOR UP TO 3 DAYS IN A SEALED CONTAINER IN THE REFRIGERATOR OR 2-3 MONTHS IN THE FREEZER. IT IS A GOOD IDEA TO FREEZE IT IN BLOCKS OF 500ML/18FL OZ/2 CUPS AND OF 100ML/3½ FL OZ/½ CUP.

Vegetable nage *If you can chop vegetables and regulate a cooker tap, you can make a good stock-base or sauce.*

Fish stock

THE BEST FISH BONES TO USE FOR STOCK, IF POSSIBLE, ARE TURBOT OR SOLE – OTHERS CAN BE TOO OILY OR STRONG IN FLAVOUR – BUT HAKE OR HADDOCK WILL DO INSTEAD. CUT OUT THE EYES AND GILLS, AND MAKE SURE ANY TRACES OF BLOOD ARE WASHED OUT. IF YOUR FISHMONGER DOESN'T HAVE SUFFICIENT BONES, YOU CAN USE TAIL PIECES OF FISH INSTEAD.

INGREDIENTS (makes about 2 litres/3½ pints/9 cups)

1 small leek, finely chopped
1 small onion, finely chopped
1 celery stick, finely chopped
½ bulb fennel, finely chopped
2 cloves garlic, unpeeled
100ml/3½ fl oz/½ cup olive oil
1.5kg/3lb 4oz fish bones, roughly chopped
300ml/½ pint/1¼ cups dry white wine
2 litres/3½ pints/9 cups cold water
2 sprigs each of parsley and thyme
½ lemon, sliced
¼ teaspoon white peppercorns

1 In a covered stockpot or large saucepan, sweat the vegetables in the oil over a medium heat for about 7 minutes until they are softened but not coloured.
2 Add the fish bones and wine, and cook until the wine has evaporated.
3 Pour in the water, which should just cover the bones. Bring to the boil and, using a ladle, skim off the scum that rises to the top.
4 When all the scum has been removed, add the fresh herbs, lemon slices and peppercorns, and simmer for about 20 minutes. Remove from the heat and allow to rest undisturbed for about 10 minutes so that the liquid can clear and settle.
5 Strain the stock by pouring the contents of the pan through a muslin-lined colander set over a large bowl or food container. Cool the strained stock, then chill or freeze until required.

STORAGE

THIS STOCK WILL KEEP FOR UP TO 7 DAYS IN A SEALED CONTAINER IN THE REFRIGERATOR, PROVIDED IT IS BOILED FOR A FEW MINUTES EVERY 3-4 DAYS. IT MAY ALSO BE FROZEN – IN USABLE AMOUNTS AS DESIRED – FOR UP TO 2 MONTHS.

Fish velouté

THE LIGHT BODY OF THIS FULL-FLAVOURED SAUCE COMES FROM THE WELL-REDUCED STOCK AND THE CREAM. THE SAUCE CAN BE MADE AHEAD OF TIME AND STORED IN THE REFRIGERATOR FOR A COUPLE OF DAYS.

INGREDIENTS (makes about 450ml/¾ pint/2 cups)

4 shallots, finely sliced
15g/½oz butter
250ml/9fl oz/1 cup dry white wine
250ml/9fl oz/1 cup Noilly Prat or dry vermouth
500ml/18fl oz/2 cups Fish Stock (above)
250ml/9fl oz/1 cup double cream
250ml/9fl oz/1 cup single cream

1 In a wide, shallow saucepan, gently sauté the shallots in the butter for about 12 minutes until very soft, yet still uncoloured.
2 Deglaze the pan with the wine and the Noilly Prat or vermouth, then boil the liquid for about 10 minutes, or until it has reduced to the consistency of a thin syrup.
3 Stir in the Fish Stock. Bring the liquid back to the boil then continue to boil it down until it reduces by about half.
4 Stir in both creams. Return the pan to the boil and simmer the sauce for about 15 minutes or until it acquires a coating consistency.
5 For an extra smooth, velvety texture, pour the sauce through a fine sieve.

Langoustine stock

THIS STOCK FORMS THE BASE OF ONE OF MY FAVOURITE RECIPES, THE CAPPUCCINO OF ROASTED LANGOUSTINE AND LENTILS (PAGE 35). IT'S A VERY VERSATILE STOCK WHICH CAN BE REDUCED TO MAKE A RAVISHING SAUCE IN ITS OWN RIGHT WHICH IS IDEAL FOR SERVING WITH RAVIOLI AND WHICH CAN ALSO BE REDUCED FURTHER AND USED AS A BASE FOR A VINAIGRETTE. AS SUCH, IT WILL MAKE A MEMORABLE DRESSING FOR ANY SALAD WHICH INCLUDES SEAWATER FISH OR SHELLFISH. YOU MAY FIND THAT YOUR FISHMONGER SELLS LANGOUSTINES UNDER THE NAME OF DUBLIN BAY PRAWNS. INSTEAD OF THROWING AWAY THEIR HEADS AFTER PEELING, RESERVE THEM FOR MAKING THIS STOCK. LOBSTER CARCASSES, CHOPPED INTO 5CM/2IN PIECES, CAN BE PUT TO THE SAME USE TO GOOD EFFECT.

1 Heat a large roasting pan on top of the cooker and add half of the oil. When hot, sauté the langoustine heads and shells if using, shaking the pan and turning the heads occasionally until they turn golden brown.

2 In another large pan, heat the remaining oil and add all of the vegetables, sautéeing them until they start to caramelize and acquire a golden colour. Add the sautéed langoustine heads.

3 Deglaze with the Cognac, then add the wine and boil until reduced by about half. Pour in the Fish Stock, water, fresh herbs and spices. Simmer the stock for about 20 minutes to reduce it down by one-third and cook out the raw flavours.

4 Strain the liquid through a muslin-lined sieve. It is now ready to use as a stock, which can be reduced again slightly for a little more concentration of flavour and to make a delicious sauce. Check the seasoning just before use.

INGREDIENTS (makes about 1 litre/ 1¾ pints/4½ cups)

100ml/3½ fl oz/½ cup olive oil
24 heads, or heads and shells, of langoustines, weighing about 500g/1lb
2 small carrots, chopped
1 onion, chopped
1 celery stick, chopped
2 cloves garlic, unpeeled
1 small bulb fennel, chopped
2 fresh tomatoes, chopped
2 teaspoons Cognac
200ml/7fl oz/⅞ cup dry white wine
500ml/18fl oz/2 cups Fish Stock (page 14)
500ml/18fl oz/2 cups cold water
1 large sprig each of tarragon, basil, thyme and coriander
½ bay leaf
2 star anise
¼ teaspoon white peppercorns
¼ teaspoon black peppercorns
¼ teaspoon coriander seeds
sea salt (optional)

STORAGE

THE STOCK AND THE SAUCE WILL KEEP FOR UP TO 2 DAYS IN THE REFRIGERATOR, OR FOR UP TO 2 MONTHS IN THE FREEZER.

Court-bouillon

A LIGHT, FRAGRANT STOCK OF VEGETABLES, HERBS AND WHITE WINE, THIS COURT-BOUILLON IS USED FOR POACHING FISH, CRABS AND VARIOUS OTHER SHELLFISH. AFTER USING IT ONCE FOR POACHING PURPOSES, IT CAN BE FROZEN AND THEN RE-USED ONCE OR TWICE AGAIN BEFORE DISCARDING.

INGREDIENTS (makes 1.5 litres/ 2¾ pints/6½ cups)

4 leeks, coarsely chopped
4 carrots, coarsely chopped
2 celery sticks, coarsely chopped
4 onions, coarsely chopped
6 shallots, coarsely chopped
2 bulbs fennel, coarsely chopped
6 cloves garlic, unpeeled
1 large sprig each of thyme, tarragon, basil and parsley
2 litres/3½ pints/9 cups cold water
¼ teaspoon white peppercorns
25g/1oz rock salt
2 lemons, sliced
4 star anise
400ml/14fl oz/1¾ cups dry white wine

1 Place the vegetables and fresh herbs in a stockpot or large saucepan. Add sufficient water to just cover the ingredients. Bring the water to the boil.
2 Add the peppercorns, salt, lemon slices, star anise and wine. Bring the liquid to the boil again, then simmer for about 30 minutes.
3 Strain the stock by pouring the contents of the pan through a muslin-lined colander set over a large bowl or food container. Discard the vegetables, herbs, spices and lemon. The Court-bouillon is now ready for use. Alternatively, chill or freeze until required.

STORAGE

COURT-BOUILLON WILL KEEP FOR UP TO 2-3 DAYS IN A SEALED CONTAINER IN THE REFRIGERATOR OR FOR 2-3 MONTHS IN THE FREEZER.

Veal stock

THE BASE FOR MANY OF MY SAUCES, VEAL STOCK HAS RICHNESS, BODY AND AN ATTRACTIVE COLOUR. VEAL BONES ARE BEST FOR THIS STOCK BECAUSE OF THEIR GELATINE AND FINE FLAVOUR; BUT YOU CAN ALSO USE BEEF BONES. THE BONES CAN BE OBTAINED FROM MANY TRADITIONAL BUTCHERS, ALTHOUGH YOU MAY NEED TO ORDER THEM IN ADVANCE. AS BOTH VEAL AND BEEF BONES TEND TO BE QUITE LARGE, ASK THE BUTCHER TO CHOP THEM UP FOR YOU SO THAT THEIR FLAVOUR CAN BE FULLY RELEASED.

INGREDIENTS (makes about 2-3 litres/3½-5¼ pints/9-13 cups)

3kg/6½lb veal or beef bones
200ml/7fl oz/⅞ cup olive oil
2 large onions, coarsely chopped
4 large carrots, coarsely chopped
3 celery sticks, coarsely chopped
½ whole head garlic, unpeeled
2 tablespoons concentrated tomato purée
350ml/12fl oz/1½ cups Madeira
350ml/12fl oz/1½ cups ruby port
10 litres/18 pints cold water
200g/7oz mushrooms
1 large Bouquet Garni (page 18)

1 Preheat the oven to 220°C/425°F/Gas Mark 7. Place the bones in a large roasting pan with half the olive oil and roast in the oven until golden brown, turning occasionally. This should take between 1-1½ hours.
2 Meanwhile, place the vegetables with the garlic in a stockpot or large saucepan with the remaining oil. Fry gently until lightly coloured, turning occasionally.

3 Stir in the tomato purée and continue cooking until everything is golden brown then pour in the Madeira and the port. Reduce the liquid by boiling gently until it acquires a syrupy consistency.

4 Once the bones have a rich colour, drain them of any fat using kitchen paper towels if necessary. Add them to the vegetables along with the water.

5 Bring the water to the boil, skim off the scum that rises using a ladle, then add the mushrooms and the Bouquet Garni. Simmer very gently for about 6 hours, skimming off any further scum that accumulates on the surface.

6 Strain the stock by pouring the contents of the pan through a muslin-lined colander set over a large bowl. Discard the bones, vegetables and Bouquet Garni.

7 Wipe out the stockpot or saucepan and return the stock to the pan. Boil down again until reduced by half. Cool and use as required.

STORAGE

The stock will keep for up to 7 days in a sealed container in the refrigerator, provided it is reboiled for a good 5 minutes every 2-3 days. The stock may also be frozen – in usable amounts as desired – for up to 2 months.

Lamb stock

Specially for use in lamb dishes and sauces. We use rib or neck of lamb bones, but shoulder or leg bones are also fine.

INGREDIENTS (makes about 2 litres/3½ pints/9 cups)

2kg/4½lb lamb rib or neck bones
100ml/3½fl oz/½ cup olive oil
1 large onion, coarsely chopped
3 large carrots, coarsely chopped
2 celery sticks, coarsely chopped
½ whole head garlic, unpeeled
250ml/9fl oz/1 cup dry white wine
1 tablespoon concentrated tomato purée
1 Bouquet Garni (page 18)
8 litres/14 pints cold water

1 Preheat the oven to 200°C/400°F/Gas Mark 6. Place the lamb bones in a large roasting tin and stir in half the oil. Roast in the oven for 50-60 minutes, turning occasionally until well browned.

2 Meanwhile, in a stockpot or a large saucepan, heat the remaining oil, and brown the vegetables for about 15 minutes, stirring occasionally.

3 Deglaze with the wine and cook until the liquid has reduced by about half. Stir in the concentrated tomato purée, Bouquet Garni and the water.

4 Remove the bones from the oven and tip into the stockpot or saucepan, being careful to avoid pouring in any of the fat or oil.

5 Gradually bring to the boil, skimming with a large spoon to remove any sediment that forms on the top.

6 Boil gently for about 4 hours or until reduced by half, still skimming occasionally.

7 Carefully pour through a muslin-lined colander set over a bowl.

8 Wipe out the stockpot or saucepan and return the stock to the pan. Boil again until reduced to about 2 litres/3½ pints/9 cups. Cool, chill and remove any fat that sets on the top. Use as required.

STORAGE

Lamb Stock will keep for up to a week in a sealed container in the refrigerator, provided it is brought to the boil for a few minutes every 3-4 days. It may also be frozen – in usable amounts as desired – for up to 2 months.

Chicken stock

A GOOD BASE STOCK, AMBER-COLOURED AND NOT TOO STRONG IN TASTE. IN THE RESTAURANT WE MAKE IT USING THE CARCASSES FROM FRESH CHICKENS, BUT YOU CAN USE BONY CHICKEN JOINTS, SUCH AS WINGS, INSTEAD. IF YOUR LOCAL BUTCHER CANNOT OBLIGE, CHINESE FOOD STORES ARE A GOOD SOURCE OF THESE JOINTS, SOLD FROZEN IN PACKS. THAW THEM WELL BEFORE USE.

1 Place the raw chicken carcasses or joints in a stockpot or large saucepan and cover with the water. Bring to the boil, skimming well with a ladle.

2 Add all the remaining ingredients, making sure they are completely submerged. Return to the boil and simmer gently for about 4½ hours, skimming frequently.

3 Strain the stock by pouring the contents of the pan through a muslin-lined colander set over a large bowl or another large saucepan. Discard the bones, vegetables and Bouquet Garni. Cool the strained stock, then chill or freeze until needed.

INGREDIENTS (makes about 3 litres/5¼ pints/13 cups)

3kg/6½lb raw chicken carcasses or about the same weight in bony chicken joints e.g. wings, drumsticks
5 litres/9 pints cold water
4 celery sticks, coarsely chopped
2 leeks, coarsely chopped
3 large onions, quartered
3 large carrots, coarsely chopped
½ whole head garlic, unpeeled
1 large sprig thyme
25g/1oz rock salt

STORAGE

THE STOCK WILL KEEP FOR UP TO 7 DAYS IN A SEALED CONTAINER IN THE REFRIGERATOR, PROVIDED IT IS REBOILED FOR A GOOD 5 MINUTES EVERY 2-3 DAYS. THE STOCK MAY ALSO BE FROZEN – IN USABLE AMOUNTS AS DESIRED – FOR UP TO 2 MONTHS.

Brown chicken stock

Some of my recipes call for a darker brown chicken stock. This is achieved simply by first browning the chicken carcasses or joints in the oven. Preheat the oven to 200°C/400°F/Gas Mark 6. Roast the chicken carcasses or joints for about 15-20 minutes, turning frequently, until dark golden brown. Drain through a colander then proceed with the recipe above.

Bouquet garni

YOU COULD JUST TIE THESE LEAVES AND SPRIGS INTO A BUNCH, THEN TOSS THE SEEDS INTO THE POT, BUT WE PREFER TO MAKE THEM INTO A NEAT PARCEL. USE THE 'BUTT' OF THE LEEK (THE OUTER TWO LEAVES) AS THE WRAPPING AND KITCHEN STRING TO HOLD IT ALL IN PLACE. A BOUQUET GARNI WILL KEEP FRESH FOR SEVERAL DAYS IF STORED IN THE REFRIGERATOR.

1 Separate out the outer 2 leaves of the white of the leek and place the celery, thyme, parsley stalks and bay leaf in the centre. Spoon in the peppercorns and coriander seeds.

2 Fold in the ends and sides of the leek and roll into a neat parcel.

3 Tie firmly in a number of places.

INGREDIENTS (for 1 Bouquet Garni)

'butt' of 1 large leek
½ celery stick
1 sprig thyme
few parsley stalks
1 bay leaf
½ teaspoon black peppercorns
½ teaspoon white peppercorns
6 coriander seeds

Dressings and sauces

MOST OF THESE DRESSINGS AND SAUCES CAN BE MADE IN LARGER AMOUNTS AND STORED IN THE REFRIGERATOR. IF YOU HAVE DIFFICULTY MEASURING SMALL AMOUNTS OF LIQUIDS, REMEMBER THAT ONE STANDARD MEASURING TABLESPOON IS ABOUT 15ML, ONE DESSERTSPOON 10ML, AND A TEASPOON 5ML.

Tapenade

WE SPREAD THIS ON PAN-FRIED FISH FILLETS SUCH AS MULLET, BUT IT CAN ALSO BE USED AS AN ALL-PURPOSE FLAVOURING OR AS A DIP FOR CROÛTES.

1 Simply place all the ingredients in a food processor or liquidizer and blend for about 2-3 minutes.

2 Spoon into clean screw-top glass jars and seal down. Store in the refrigerator and use as required.

INGREDIENTS (makes enough to fill a medium glass jar)

200g/7oz/1 cup pitted black olives
40g/1½ oz/2 tablespoons anchovies
20g/¾ oz/¼ cup capers, rinsed
1 clove garlic, crushed
1 tablespoon extra-virgin olive oil

Pesto

HOMEMADE PESTO HAS A MUCH CLEANER, FRESHER TASTE THAN THE READY-MADE VARIETIES. IT IS EXCELLENT WITH PASTA OR AS A GARNISH FOR SOUPS.

1 Place the pine kernels, garlic and Parmesan into a food processor or liquidizer and process until finely ground.

2 With the motor still running, feed the basil leaves into the machine through the funnel, then slowly trickle in the oil. Blend until smooth and creamy. Store in clean screw-top glass jars in the refrigerator.

INGREDIENTS (makes enough to fill a medium glass jar)

50g/2oz/½ cup pine kernels
50g/2oz garlic cloves, peeled and stalk ends trimmed
50g/2oz/¼ cup finely grated Parmesan cheese
30g/1¼oz basil leaves
125ml/4fl oz/½ cup extra-virgin olive oil

Basic salad vinaigrette

SHERRY VINEGAR PROVIDES DEPTH OF FLAVOUR, AND OLIVE OIL BLENDED WITH GROUNDNUT OIL GIVES A LIGHT CONSISTENCY TO OUR VINAIGRETTE.

1 Pour the vinegar into a bowl or jug. Add a good pinch each of salt and pepper, and, using a whisk, stir until dissolved.

2 Add the oils and lemon juice then whisk again to form a light emulsion. Taste for seasoning and use as required. Leftover Vinaigrette can be stored in a screw-top glass jar and shaken prior to use to emulsify it again.

INGREDIENTS (makes 350ml/12fl oz/1½ cups)

50ml/2fl oz/¼ cup sherry vinegar
250ml/9fl oz/1 cup extra-virgin olive oil
50ml/2fl oz/¼ cup groundnut oil
juice of ½ lemon
sea salt and ground white pepper

Truffle cream vinaigrette

OUR ACCOMPANIMENT FOR THE MOSAIC OF RABBIT WITH CABBAGE AND CÈPES (PAGE 67), BUT EQUALLY STUNNING TOSSED INTO SALAD OF MIXED SALAD LEAVES (PAGE 54), OR POURED OVER HOT NEW POTATOES AND SIMPLE POACHED FISH. TRUFFLE OIL CAN BE FOUND IN GOOD DELICATESSENS.

INGREDIENTS (makes about 350ml/12fl oz/1½ cups)

150ml/¼ pint/¾ cup extra-virgin olive oil
50ml/2fl oz/¼ cup groundnut oil
50ml/2fl oz/¼ cup truffle oil
2 tablespoons sherry vinegar
50ml/2fl oz/¼ cup double cream
sea salt and ground white pepper

1 In a bowl or jug, whisk together the oils, vinegar and a good pinch each of salt and pepper.

2 Lightly whip the cream until it just begins to hold soft peaks, then fold it into the Vinaigrette. Taste for seasoning and use as required. Leftover dressing can be stored in a screw-top glass jar.

Sauce vierge

A CORIANDER AND BASIL DRESSING WHICH MAKES AN EXCELLENT MATCH FOR RED MULLET, SCALLOPS OR FRESH PAN-FRIED TUNA.

INGREDIENTS (for 6)

6 basil leaves
6 large coriander leaves
6 coriander seeds
50ml/2fl oz/¼cup extra-virgin olive oil
2 tablespoons fresh lemon juice
1 heaped teaspoon Shallot Confit (page 94)
½ teaspoon balsamic vinegar
sea salt and ground white pepper

1 Shred the basil and coriander leaves into fine julienne strips, and crush the coriander seeds using a pestle and mortar.

2 Heat the oil and lemon juice very gently in a small saucepan then add the Shallot Confit, herbs, crushed berries, vinegar and seasoning. Stir briefly, then remove from the heat and leave to infuse for at least 5 and up to 30 minutes. Serve the sauce warm, at room temperature or chilled.

Sauce antiboise

A CLASSIC FRENCH MEDITERRANEAN SAUCE WITH A WONDERFUL FRESH TASTE TO COMPLEMENT ROASTED FISH OR LAMB, BUT EQUALLY GOOD TOSSED INTO PASTA AND RICE SALADS OR MIXED INTO HOT NEW POTATOES.

INGREDIENTS (makes about 450ml/¾ pint/1⅞ cups)

3 large tomatoes, weighing a total of about 400g/14oz
3 large shallots, finely chopped
1 small clove garlic, crushed
200ml/7fl oz/⅞ cup olive oil
6 basil leaves
6 large coriander leaves
6 sprigs tarragon
juice of ½ lemon
sea salt and freshly ground black pepper

1 Dip the tomatoes first into boiling water, then into cold, and peel their skins away. Quarter, remove the seeds and cut into very fine dice; set aside.

2 In a heavy-based pan, sweat the shallots and garlic gently in the oil for about 5 minutes or until softened, but still uncoloured.

3 Meanwhile, shred the herbs into fine julienne strips. Mix them into the shallots and leave to infuse off the heat for 5 minutes.

4 Stir in the tomato dice and heat gently. Add the lemon juice and seasoning to taste. Serve hot. The sauce can be stored in the refrigerator for several days and reheated as necessary.

Rouille

A FRENCH EGG AND OLIVE OIL SAUCE TO SERVE SPREAD ON ROUNDS OF FRENCH BREAD, THEN FLOATED IN FISH SOUPS, SUCH AS BOUILLABAISSE WITH SAFFRON NEW POTATOES (PAGE 114). ALTERNATIVELY, TRY IT WITH ROASTED SARDINES OR GRILLED SALMON.

INGREDIENTS (makes about 300ml/½ pint /1¼ cups, enough for 4)

1 potato, weighing about 85g/3oz
2 eggs, hard boiled
2 egg yolks
2 cloves garlic, crushed
3 pinches of saffron strands
200ml/7fl oz/⅞ cup olive oil
sea salt and freshly ground black pepper

1 Boil the potato, then peel and mash it to a smooth purée. Set aside to cool.

2 Peel the hard-boiled eggs, chop them roughly and rub through a metal sieve using your fingers or the back of a spoon.

3 Put the potato and egg into a bowl with the egg yolks, garlic and seasoning. Crush the saffron strands into the mixture and blend well.

4 Trickle in the oil very slowly, beating steadily with a wooden spoon as if making a mayonnaise, until you have a thick, glossy sauce. Correct the seasoning and serve.

Red wine sauce

A FULL-BODIED SAUCE THAT IS BRILLIANT FOR SERVING NOT JUST WITH MEAT BUT ALSO WITH 'MEATY' FISH, SUCH AS ROASTED MONKFISH (PAGE 113) AND CONFIT OF TUNA (PAGE 107). I OFTEN SERVE FISH WITH MEAT-STOCK BASED SAUCES.

INGREDIENTS (makes about 400ml/14fl oz/1¾ cups)

800ml/1 pint 10fl oz/3½ cups Chicken Stock (page 18)
1 x 75cl bottle red wine
2 tablespoons olive oil
8 shallots, sliced
1 teaspoon five-spice powder
12 black peppercorns
1 sprig thyme
1 small bay leaf
1 tablespoon sherry vinegar
sea salt and freshly ground black pepper

1 Have ready the Chicken Stock and set aside. In another saucepan boil the bottle of wine until it is rich and syrupy and reduced to about enough to fill one large wine glass.

2 In yet another saucepan, heat the oil and sauté the shallots together with the five-spice powder, peppercorns, thyme and bay leaf until caramelized – about 10 minutes. Deglaze with the vinegar then pour in the red wine 'syrup'.

3 Stir in the Chicken Stock, bring to the boil then boil hard for about 20 minutes to reduce by about half, skimming occasionally with a ladle as required.

4 Pour this at least twice through a sieve lined with wet muslin or a fine cloth to remove all the vegetables and herb particles until you have a smooth sauce. Season as required.

Jus de fraises

CONSISTING SOLELY OF THE PURE JUICE OF RIPE STRAWBERRIES – WITH NO ADDED SUGAR – THIS FRESH-TASTING DESSERT SAUCE IS THE IDEAL COMPLEMENT FOR CRÈME BRÛLÉE OR ICE-CREAMS.

INGREDIENTS (makes about 300ml/½ pint /1¼ cups)

500g/1lb 2oz ripe strawberries, hulled and sliced

1 Place the strawberries in a heatproof bowl. Cover with cling film and set the bowl over a pan of simmering water for 25-30 minutes, or until the juice has drained fully from the fruit.

2 Meanwhile, line a sieve with damp muslin or with a damp, thin tea towel and place over a bowl.

3 Remove the heatproof bowl from the heat and pour its contents through the sieve. When all the juice has dripped through the sieve, discard the fruit pulp and chill until required.

Crème pâtissière

A MARVELLOUSLY USEFUL BASE FOR COLD OR HOT RECIPES. USE IT AS A CREAM FILLING FOR FRUIT TARTS AND FLANS OR AS A SOUFFLÉ BASE. BECAUSE A SINGLE BATCH CAN HAVE MULTIPLE USES, IT IS WORTH MAKING MORE THAN YOU NEED, ESPECIALLY AS IT WILL KEEP, IF WELL COVERED, FOR UP TO A WEEK IN THE REFRIGERATOR.

INGREDIENTS (makes about 600ml/1 pint/2½ cups)

600ml/1 pint/2½ cups milk
75g/2¾ oz/⅓ cup caster sugar
6 egg yolks
90g/3oz/½ cup 2 tablespoons plain flour
1 dessertspoon cornflour

1 Put the milk to boil in a large saucepan.

2 In a large bowl, whisk together the sugar and egg yolks until the mixture is pale. Gradually work in the two flours, mixing well until the ingredients are blended smoothly.

3 When the milk starts to boil, pour half of it in a thin stream on to the yolk mixture, whisking well as you pour. When it is well blended, whisk in the remaining hot milk in the same way.

4 Return the mixture to the saucepan and set it over a low to medium heat. Cook gently, stirring occasionally, for up to 2 minutes until it starts to leave the sides of the pan. It should now be smooth and thick. Cool for a few minutes, then spoon back into the bowl. Cover the surface tightly with cling film to prevent a skin from forming. When cold, use as required.

MAKING SMALL QUANTITIES:

IT IS HARD TO MAKE CRÈME PÂTISSIÈRE IN VERY SMALL QUANTITIES. IF A RECIPE CALLS FOR A QUARTER OF THE AMOUNT GIVEN HERE, MAKE A HALF-QUANTITY AND DIVIDE IT INTO TWO. IF A RECIPE CALLS FOR ONE-THIRD, THEN USE THE FOLLOWING AMOUNTS:

200ml/7fl oz/⅞ cup milk
2 tablespoons caster sugar
2 egg yolks
2 tablespoons plain flour
1 teaspoon cornflour

Stock syrup

USEFUL FOR A GREAT MANY DESSERT METHODS SUCH AS POACHING FRUIT, COATING DRIED FRUIT SUCH AS APPLE TUILES (PAGE 184) OR PROVIDING A BASE FOR FRUIT SALADS AND FRUIT TERRINES. BECAUSE OF ITS HIGH SUGAR CONTENT, STOCK SYRUP KEEPS WELL IN THE REFRIGERATOR FOR AT LEAST 3 MONTHS. IT IS ALWAYS USEFUL TO HAVE A BATCH TO HAND.

INGREDIENTS (makes about 1.5 litres/2¾ pints/6½ cups)

550g/1¼lb/2¾ cups granulated sugar
1 litre/1¾ pints/4½ cups cold water
grated zest of 1 lemon

1 Put the sugar, water and lemon zest into a heavy-based saucepan. Bring slowly to the boil, stirring occasionally. When all the granules of sugar have dissolved, boil the syrup for about 5 minutes.

2 Cool, and store in the refrigerator in a sealed container until required.

Pâte à bombe

I USE THIS AS THE BASE FOR MANY OF MY ICE-CREAMS AS IT PROVIDES THEM WITH LIGHTNESS AND STABILITY. THE METHOD IS SIMILAR TO THAT USED FOR MAKING LEMON CURD – THE INGREDIENTS ARE STIRRED IN A HEAT-PROOF BOWL SET IN A BAIN-MARIE OF SIMMERING WATER UNTIL THE MIXTURE IS THICK ENOUGH TO HOLD A WOODEN SPOON UPRIGHT.

INGREDIENTS (makes about 700ml/1¼ pints/3 cups)

8 egg yolks
150ml/¼ pint/¾ cup cold water
200g/7oz/1 cup caster sugar

1 Put a saucepan of water on to boil. Meanwhile, in a small to medium heatproof bowl that will fit inside the saucepan, whisk the yolks, water and sugar until the ingredients are smoothly blended.

2 When the water starts to boil, adjust to a simmer and set the bowl inside the saucepan, ensuring that the water level just reaches the height of the mixture.

3 Cook, stirring frequently, for up to one hour or until the mixture has thickened to the point at which you can stand a wooden spoon upright in the centre. During cooking, check the water level from time to time and top it up with more boiling water as necessary.

4 Off the heat remove the bowl, allow the mixture to cool slightly then rub it through a fine sieve with the back of a spoon or a ladle. Using an electric whisk, beat the mixture until it is cool and has become light and fluffy. Use as required.

Meringue

Italian meringue

THIS IS A STABLE TYPE OF MERINGUE WHICH HOLDS ITS VOLUME AFTER WHISKING, MAKING IT IDEAL FOR USE IN SOUFFLÉS. THE SUGAR IS MADE INTO A SYRUP, BOILED TO THE HARD BALL STAGE (FOR WHICH YOU WILL NEED A SUGAR THERMOMETER), THEN WHISKED INTO WHIPPED EGG WHITES. LIQUID GLUCOSE, AN INERT SUGAR WHICH PREVENTS SUCROSE SUGAR FROM HARDENING, CAN BE BOUGHT FROM CHEMISTS.

INGREDIENTS (for about 2 litres/3½ pints/9 cups)

350g/12oz/1¾ cups caster sugar
2 teaspoons liquid glucose
100ml/3½fl oz/½ cup cold water
6 egg whites

1 Put the sugar, glucose and water into a heavy-based saucepan and place over a gentle heat, stirring occasionally, until the sugar and glucose have dissolved. When clear, boil the syrup to the soft ball stage – that is, when it reaches 116°C/240°F – which takes about 5 minutes.
2 Meanwhile, in a large mixing bowl or electric stand mixer, whisk the egg whites to the soft peak stage and turn off the machine. Let the sugar reach 121°C/250°F – the hard ball stage – which takes a minute or two. Immediately remove the syrup from the heat.
3 Turn the mixer with the egg whites back on to a slow speed.
4 Slowly pour the sugar syrup down the side of the bowl into the whites, and continue to whisk until tepid. Use as required.

NOTE:

IF YOU DO NOT HAVE AN ELECTRIC MIXER, MIX THE EGG WHITES WITH A BALLOON WHISK TO THE SOFT PEAK STAGE BEFORE POURING THE SYRUP INTO THE BOWL.

French meringue

THIS MERINGUE NEEDS TO BE USED QUICKLY AS THE SUGAR IS NOT DISSOLVED AND SO BREAKS DOWN WHEN LEFT TO STAND. IT IS QUITE UNLIKE ITALIAN MERINGUE, WHICH IS STABLE BECAUSE IT IS MADE WITH SYRUP.

INGREDIENTS (makes about 1 litre/1¾ pints/4½ cups)

4 egg whites
pinch of salt
250g/9oz/1¼ cups caster sugar

1 Put the egg whites into a clean, greasefree bowl with a pinch of salt and a pinch of the sugar.
2 Using an electric whisk, beat slowly at first to form a froth then gradually increase the speed to full power.
3 Beat to firm peak stage making sure the whites are not overbeaten, dry or grainy. Slowly add the remaining sugar while the beaters are still running. The mixture should become smooth and glossy. Use immediately according to recipe requirements.

Pastry

Puff pastry

TASTING HOMEMADE PUFF PASTRY IS QUITE A REVELATION! IT IS FAR MOISTER THAN BOUGHT PASTRY YET STILL LIGHT AND FLAKY WITH A FULL, BUTTERY TASTE. ONCE YOU HAVE PRACTISED MAKING IT TWO OR THREE TIMES, IT BECOMES SURPRISINGLY EASY TO DO, AND IT'S HARD TO TURN BACK TO BUYING READY-MADE SUBSTITUTES.

INGREDIENTS (makes 1.2kg/2lb 12oz)

500g/1lb 2oz/3⅓ cups plain flour
good pinch of salt
500g/1lb 2oz/4½ sticks unsalted butter, cut into chunks
1 teaspoon white wine vinegar
about 300ml/½ pint/1¼ cups ice-cold water

1 Weigh out 450g/1lb of the flour into a bowl and mix in the salt. Rub in 50g/2oz of the butter until the mixture looks like fine breadcrumbs. This can be done in a food mixer, a food processor or by hand.

2 Add the vinegar, then trickle in the ice-cold water, mixing with a table knife until the ingredients come together in a smooth dough. You may not need all the water, or you may need a little extra. It is hard to be specific. Again this can be done in a machine or by hand. Knead gently then wrap in cling film.

3 Blend the remaining 50g/2oz of the flour with the rest of the butter. This is best done by machine, processing until the mixture is smooth and just comes together. Spoon the butter mixture out onto a large sheet of cling film and shape into a rectangle about 14 x 20cm/5½ x 8in. Wrap up completely in the cling film and chill both the dough and butter packages in the refrigerator for 20 minutes.

4 On a lightly floured work surface, roll out the dough to a rectangle almost twice the size of the butter mixture (approximately 25 x 35cm/10 x 14in). Try to keep the edges as straight as possible and the corners well angled. If necessary, tease the dough into shape.

5 Place the butter mixture down the long side of the dough, fold over the dough to enclose the butter completely then pinch the edges to seal.

6 Dust off any surplus flour with a dry pastry-brush, then carefully roll out the dough in one direction only until it is about three times the length, making sure none of the butter breaks through.

7 Fold the dough neatly into three, bringing the top third down and placing the bottom third over it. Give the dough a quarter-turn and roll out again. Dust the board and rolling pin lightly with flour and roll out again to a long rectangle the same size as before, keeping the edges and corners neat.

8 Fold into thirds as before, wrap in cling film and leave to rest in the refrigerator for 20 minutes. Unwrap, then, with the smooth, folded edge to the side, roll out again into a long rectangle as before.

▶

A FEW HELPFUL HINTS:

- TAKE THE BUTTER OUT OF THE REFRIGERATOR ABOUT AN HOUR BEFORE YOU USE IT.
- WHEN ROLLING OUT THE DOUGH, ALWAYS KEEP THE EDGES AS STRAIGHT AS YOU CAN AND THE CORNERS NEAT AND TRUE, TUGGING THEM GENTLY INTO PLACE IF YOU CAN'T QUITE MASTER THE ROLLING.
- IT IS IMPORTANT THAT THE LAYERS OF BUTTER ARE ROLLED EVENLY INTO THE DOUGH AND CAREFUL NEAT ROLLING IS THE BEST METHOD FOR ENSURING THIS. SO ALWAYS ROLL AND FOLD IN THE SAME DIRECTION (GENERALLY BOTTOM TO TOP), AND GIVE THE DOUGH JUST A QUARTER-TURN EACH TIME, AGAIN IN THE SAME DIRECTION, NORMALLY ANTI-CLOCKWISE.

9 Fold again in three, give the dough a quarter-turn, ensuring the folded edge is still on the same side as before, and repeat the rolling and folding. Give another quarter-turn and fold into thirds, then fold again immediately so that you have a double thickness of pastry. Wrap in cling film and chill again for 20 minutes.

10 If making the pastry ahead, you can freeze the dough at this stage, dividing it in half or quarters according to the recipe. If, however, you intend to use the dough straight away, then roll it out twice more, rolling, folding and turning as before. The butter will have been rolled into wafer-thin layers between the dough; this is what causes it to rise in light, crisp layers. For specific baking times and temperatures, check each individual recipe.

Rich sweet pastry

THIS SWEET, VANILLA-SCENTED PASTRY CAN BE MADE IN AN ELECTRIC MIXER THEN DIVIDED INTO BATCHES OF 250G/9OZ OR 500G/1LB 2OZ. ANY LEFTOVER PASTRY CAN BE FROZEN.

INGREDIENTS (makes 1 kg/2lb 4oz)

250g/9oz/2⅓ sticks unsalted butter, softened at room temperature
180g/6oz/⅞ cup caster sugar
4 vanilla pods
2 x size 2 eggs, beaten
500g/1lb 2oz/3⅓ cups plain flour
¼ teaspoon salt

1 Mix the butter and sugar in an electric mixer until smooth but not fluffy. Slit open the vanilla pods, scrape out the seeds and add them to the mixture.

2 Gradually add the eggs, one by one, watching that they don't curdle. Stop the machine once or twice and scrape down the mixture.

3 Sift together the flour and salt in a large bowl. Turn the machine down to its lowest speed and spoon in the flour in stages. As soon as the mixture clings together as a crumbly dough, stop the machine, remove the dough and knead it lightly by hand to a smooth, round ball.

4 Divide the mixture into batches according to the recipe required.

5 Wrap any leftover pastry in cling film and store in the freezer where it will keep for several weeks.

Making fresh pasta

ALTHOUGH MANY OF MY RECIPES CALL FOR 200-250G/7-9OZ PASTA DOUGH, IT'S EASIER, TIMEWISE, TO MAKE A COMPLETE BATCH AND USE THE REMAINDER TO MAKE YOUR OWN TAGLIATELLE OR CANNELLONI SHEETS. THESE CAN BE INTERLEAVED WITH FREEZER TISSUE WRAP AND FROZEN. DON'T FREEZE THE DOUGH IN A BALL AS IT FORMS A DRY SKIN AND IS THEN DIFFICULT TO ROLL OUT. ROLLING OUT PASTA IS EASIEST WITH A PARTNER.

INGREDIENTS (makes 800g/1lb 12oz)

550g/1lb 4oz/4 cups plain flour

generous pinch of salt

4 eggs

6 egg yolks

2 tablespoons olive oil

Pasta dough

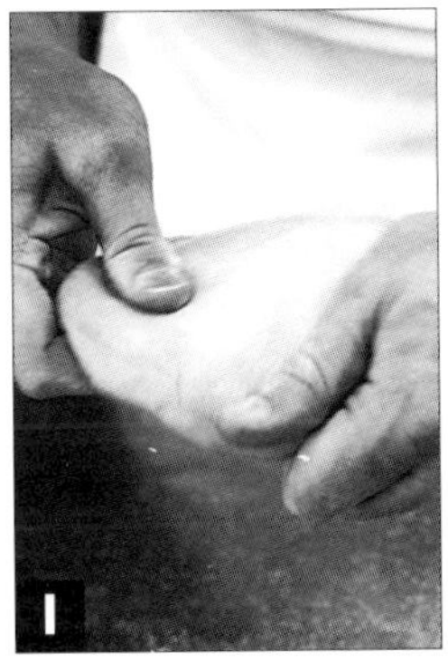

1 Sift the flour and salt together and place in a food processor along with the eggs, yolks and oil. Process until the mixture starts to come together in coarse crumbs. Stop the machine and press a small amount of the mixture together in your fingers. The mixture should not crack, but if it does process it again for a few seconds. Tip the mixture out onto a board and knead well until you have a smooth, firm ball of dough. It should feel soft but not sticky. Wrap the dough in cling film and allow to rest for an hour or two.

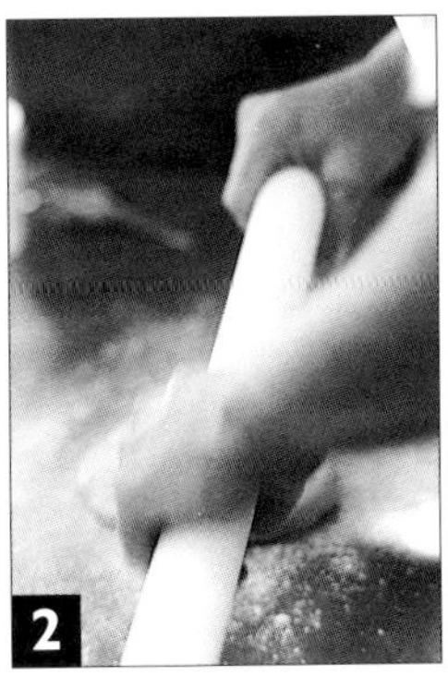

2 Divide the dough ball into eight equal pieces and knead each piece again until smooth. Taking a piece at a time, roll out each one in turn with a rolling pin on a lightly floured board until you have a rectangle about 5mm/¼in thick.

3–4 Feed each rectangle of dough through the pasta machine several times starting with the mechanism adjusted to the thickest setting (i.e. with the rollers widest apart) and adjusting the setting by one notch each time, finishing with the thinnest setting. You are now ready to cut, fill and shape your pasta, according to the individual recipe.

Making fresh pasta *I make fresh pasta by hand twice a day for ravioli, tortellini and tagliatelle to serve either as starters or in soups.*

Tortellini

1 Prepare your filling according to the recipe. You will probably need about half the quantity of Pasta Dough rolled out as described in the basic recipe, allowing for some wastage. Prepare some egg wash by beating 1 egg yolk with a pinch of salt and 2 teaspoons of water, then set aside. Using a 9cm/3½in round cutter, stamp out as many circles as you require tortellini.

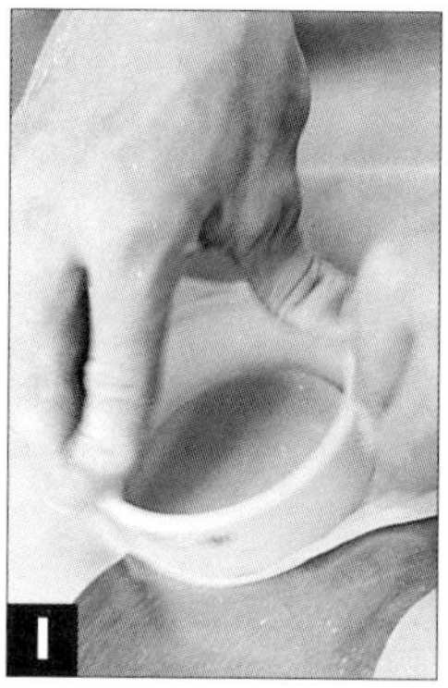
1

2

3

2-3 Press a ball of filling onto one side of each pasta disc. Using a pastry-brush, brush round the edges of each pasta disc with the beaten egg wash.

4-5 Fold over to make a semi-circle. Press the edges well to seal, making sure there are no air pockets or tears.

4

5

6–8 Take each semi-circle in your hand and curl the two tips of the straight edge around your index finger, pressing well to seal. Then turn the edges up to form a 'brim' like a hat. Repeat with the remaining dough and filling.

6

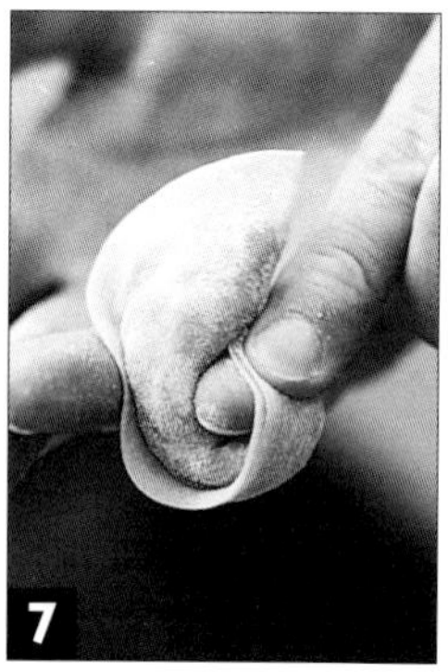
7

8

BLANCHING PASTA IN ADVANCE

9–10 Blanch homemade pasta in boiling salted water, allowing 2 minutes for tortellini and ravioli, and 30 seconds for tagliatelle. Drain and immerse in ice-cold water until cold. Drain again. Wrap in cling film and chill until required. Reheat in a little boiling water and butter for 1-2 minutes. Alternatively, cook pasta for one minute longer than the times given above, drain, toss with a little butter and serve immediately.

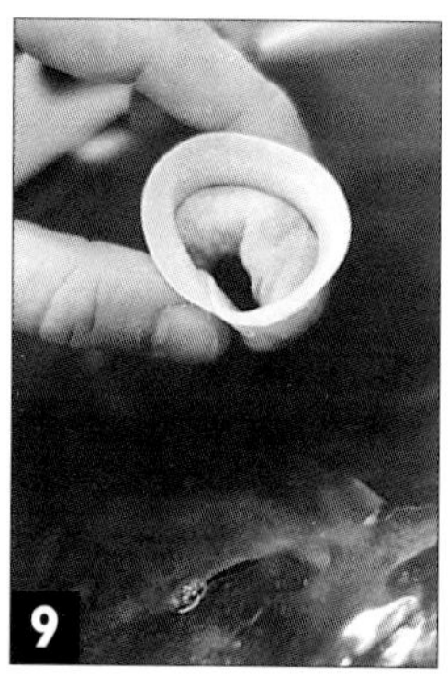
9

10

Tortellini

Tagliatelle

1 Prepare the Pasta Dough (page 27) and roll out to the thinnest setting. Ideally, allow the sheets to dry out for about 10 minutes by hanging them over the backs of clean chairs.

2 Dust the sheets lightly with flour. Fix the special noodle cutters into the pasta machine. Feed in the first sheet of dough with one hand, using the other to turn the handle. As the pasta strands emerge, stop turning at intervals, spreading the noodles out on the other side to prevent them sticking.

3 When you've finished cutting the first sheet, lift up the noodles in one hand and twirl them down into a nest on a tray. Leave to dry out for about 10 minutes.

4 Blanch and refresh the tagliatelle (page 28), then continue with the individual recipe.

Ravioli

1–2 Prepare the filling according to your recipe. Generally, you will need about half the quantity of Pasta Dough rolled out to the thinnest setting on your pasta machine. Using a 10cm/4in round cutter, cut out 2 discs for each ravioli. Press the filling into small balls and place on half the pasta discs. Brush round the edges with egg wash as for tortellini and place a second disc on top of each.

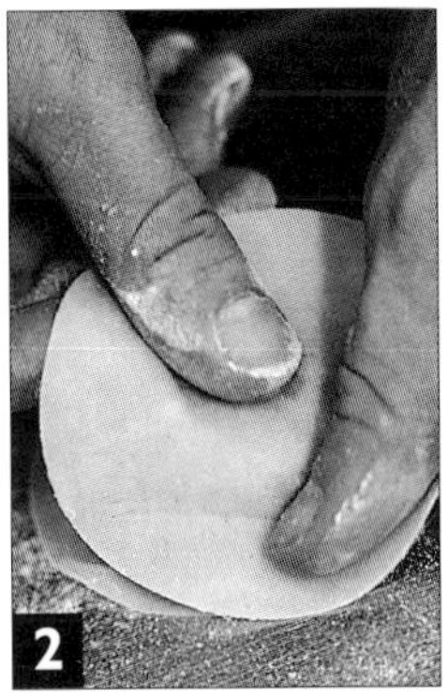

3 Seal the edges of the pasta discs by pinching them firmly together. You will need to stretch the dough so that it extends to the edges, moulding it around the filling so there are no air gaps or tears.

4 Take a crimped cutter one size smaller than the rounds, cut the parcels into neat ravioli, then peel off the excess dough from around the edges.

5 Blanch and refresh the ravioli (page 28), then continue with the individual recipe.

Tagliatelle and ravioli

Soups

I love making soups at any time of the year – whether to serve hot or chilled. The essence of a good soup is to excite the palate: certainly, I don't see a soup just as a sea to carry a few pieces of floating debris.

Our soups come in many guises: first as an *amuse-gueule* – maybe a little chilled Cucumber Gazpacho (page 46), a clear Tomato Consommé (page 49) or perhaps a light frothy Cappuccino, served in tiny espresso cups to tantalize the tastebuds. Then there are soups that resemble light, main meals with lobster claws, or prettily 'turned' vegetables resting in a light Fish Velouté (page 14).

Even the simplest of our soups bears an enhancing garnish. For example, the silky, puréed Broccoli Soup (page 50) has a special touch of baby ravioli; and my favourite Cappuccino of Haricots Blancs with Morels (page 32) is topped with a few delicate shavings of truffle.

But the starting point of all my soups is natural flavour. For many of them, this means beginning with a well-rounded stock that has been reduced to concentrate the essence of flavours. For other soups, I use a lighter Vegetable Nage (page 13) so as not to overpower the flavour of the main ingredients; and in one, the Broccoli Soup, the 'broth' is simply water.

Cappuccino of haricots blancs with morels

A LIGHT, FROTHY SOUP IN WHICH A FINE PURÉE OF HARICOT BEANS GIVES FLAVOUR AND BODY, WHILE TRUFFLE OIL AND MORELS ADD AROMATIC LUXURY. THE CAPPUCCINO-LIKE FROTH IS MADE BY WHISKING WITH A SPECIAL ELECTRIC BAMIX (SEE PAGE 189 FOR SUPPLIER), ALTHOUGH A DOMESTIC MULTI-BLENDER WILL GIVE SIMILAR RESULTS. ADDING ICE-COLD BUTTER IS THE SECRET OF PRODUCING A GOOD FROTH FOR CAPPUCCINO SAUCES AND SOUPS.

INGREDIENTS (for 6)

800ml/1 pint 6fl oz/3½ cups either Chicken Stock (page 18) or Vegetable Nage (page 13)
250g/9oz/1 cup small white dried haricot beans, soaked overnight
1 small onion, peeled
1 carrot, peeled
1 fresh Bouquet Garni (page 18)
100g/3½oz/1½ cups fresh morels or other wild mushrooms, sliced if large
50g/2oz/½ stick butter plus an extra knob of ice-cold butter for serving
1-2 teaspoons truffle oil
150ml/¼ pint/⅔ cup double cream
a few fine slices of fresh truffle (optional)
sea salt and freshly ground black pepper

1 Have ready the Chicken Stock or Vegetable Nage. Drain the soaked beans and transfer them to a large saucepan. Cover by about 5cm/2in with lightly salted cold water. Add the onion, carrot and Bouquet Garni, then bring to the boil.

2 Boil for 10 minutes then lower the heat to a simmer and cook for a further 25-30 minutes or until the beans are just soft.

3 Using a slotted spoon, remove about 100g/3oz of the beans and reserve for the garnish. Continue cooking the remainder for a further 10 minutes or until they are very soft.

4 Drain, discard the onion, carrot and Bouquet Garni and blend the beans to a fine purée in a food processor or liquidizer. For absolute perfection, rub the purée through a sieve with the back of a ladle, but this is not vital.

5 Clean out the saucepan and add either the Chicken Stock or the Vegetable Nage. Boil for 5 minutes to reduce the liquid.

6 For the garnish, sauté the mushrooms briefly in the butter until just cooked, then stir in half of the truffle oil.

7 Using a Bamix or a hand-held electric multi-blender, mix the reduced stock into the bean purée until it is smooth, then whisk in the cream and the remaining truffle oil.

8 Divide the reserved beans and mushrooms between warmed soup plates or cappuccino cups. Check the seasoning of the soup, then reheat to boiling point. Using the Bamix or blender, whisk in the ice-cold butter and froth up the soup.

9 Distribute the soup over the beans and morels, frothing it up as you work to prevent it losing its airy appearance. Garnish with the fine slices of fresh truffle if using and serve instantly.

Cappuccino of haricots

blancs with morels

Cappuccino of roasted

Cappuccino of roasted langoustine and lentils

LIKE HARICOT BLANCS, THE LITTLE BLUE-GREEN FRENCH PUY LENTILS PRODUCE A FINE LIGHT SOUP AND ALSO MAKE AN INSPIRED MATCH WITH LANGOUSTINES. SERVE THIS SOUP IN SMALL BOWLS AND, JUST BEFORE SERVING, FROTH THE SOUP WITH A BAMIX (SEE PAGE 189 FOR SUPPLIER), OR SIMILAR DOMESTIC MULTI-BLENDER, FOR TRUE CAPPUCCINO STYLE.

INGREDIENTS (for 6)

150g/5oz/¾ cup Puy lentils
1 small carrot, peeled
½ onion, peeled
1 large fresh Bouquet Garni (page 18)
1 litre/1¾ pints/4½ cups Langoustine Stock (page 15) or Fish Stock (page 14)
2 teaspoons double cream
1 teaspoon truffle oil
a little olive oil, for sautéeing
12 medium langoustines, shelled and cleaned
25g/1oz/¼ stick ice-cold unsalted butter, diced
sprigs of parsley or chervil
sea salt and freshly ground black pepper

1 Wash the lentils well by placing them in a sieve beneath cold running water. Transfer to a saucepan, just cover with cold water then add the carrot, onion and Bouquet Garni.

2 Bring to the boil then simmer for about 20 minutes or until quite soft. Drain, and discard the vegetables and Bouquet Garni. In a food processor or liquidizer blend the lentils to a fine purée, and set aside.

3 Put the Langoustine or Fish Stock into another saucepan and bring to the boil. Stir in the lentil purée and reheat until it just starts to thicken, then stop – otherwise the mixture will not froth to a cappuccino later. Stir in the cream and the truffle oil.

4 In a sauté pan, heat the olive oil then sauté the langoustines for about 3 minutes, turning frequently to colour them all over. Divide them between warmed soup bowls.

5 Check the seasoning, then froth up with a Bamix or similar device, adding the diced butter as you whisk. Pour over the langoustines in the bowls, garnish with the parsley or chervil sprigs and serve immediately.

langoustine and lentils

Watercress soup with poached oysters

AN ALL-SEASON FAVOURITE, WATERCRESS SOUP IS A POPULAR BRITISH DISH SERVED HOT IN WINTER OR LIGHTLY CHILLED IN SUMMER. HERE, I SERVE IT HOT AND GIVE IT A TOUCH OF LUXURY WITH POACHED OYSTERS – SO EASY, SO SIMPLE AND SO CLASSY.

1 Trim the watercress of its stalks. Discard the stalks, then wash the leaves twice. Drain well.

2 Put the water and salt to boil in one pan, and heat the oil in a second, larger pan.

3 Just as the oil starts to get very hot, carefully add the watercress leaves and stir continuously as they begin to wilt.

4 When the watercress has reduced by about two-thirds in volume, add the potatoes and stir well. Pour in the boiling salted water from the other pan. Return to the boil, then simmer for 6–7 minutes, or until the potatoes have softened.

5 Transfer the vegetables and liquid to a food processor or liquidizer and blend to a smooth purée. Pass the purée through a sieve using the back of a ladle. If cooking ahead, cool down the purée as quickly as possible by standing the pan in a bowl of iced water. This helps preserve the colour of the soup.

6 Just prior to serving, prise open the oysters using an oyster knife or one with a rigid, short, sharp blade (right). Save their juices and drain into a small saucepan. Bring the juices to a gentle boil, then add the oysters and poach for just 5 seconds so they are lightly cooked.

7 Return the soup purée to the saucepan and bring back to the boil. Place an oyster in each warmed soup plate. Add the oyster juices to the soup, check the seasoning and pour the soup over the oysters. Serve immediately.

INGREDIENTS (for 6)

800g/1lb 12oz watercress
1 litre/1¾ pints/4½ cups cold water
1 tablespoon salt
2 tablespoons olive oil
150g/5oz potatoes, thinly sliced
6 medium to large oysters
freshly ground black pepper

OPENING AN OYSTER

USE ONLY OYSTERS THAT ARE TIGHTLY SHUT AS THIS MEANS THEY ARE STILL FRESH. HOLD THE OYSTER FIRMLY WITH ITS FLAT SHELL UPPERMOST AND WRAPPED IN A THICK TEA TOWEL TO PREVENT SLIPPING. USING A SPECIAL OYSTER KNIFE OR SHORT, FIRM-BLADED KNIFE, INSERT THE POINT BETWEEN THE TWO SHELLS NEXT TO THE HINGE. TWIST THE KNIFE UNTIL THE HINGE BREAKS AND YOU CAN PRISE APART THE SHELLS. IMMEDIATELY SLICE THROUGH THE MUSCLE ATTACHING THE OYSTER TO THE SHELL AND FLIP THE FLESH OUT ONTO A PAPER TOWEL. TIP THE JUICES FROM THE SHELLS INTO A SMALL CUP AND RESERVE FOR LATER USE.

Soupe de poissons provençale

A LIGHTER SOUP THAN BOUILLABAISSE, THIS CLASSIC SOUP FROM THE SOUTH OF FRANCE SEEMS TO BE MADE ALL OVER EUROPE WHEREVER IT IS POSSIBLE TO BUY A GOOD VARIETY OF SMALL MEDITERRANEAN FISH. INDEED, THE SECRET OF THIS SOUP IS TO USE AS MANY DIFFERENT FISH AS YOU CAN FIND. YOU WILL NEED A STRONG FOOD PROCESSOR FOR THIS RECIPE. SERVE WITH FRESHLY MADE CROÛTONS (I LOVE LOTS OF CROÛTONS), HOMEMADE ROUILLE (PAGE 21) AND PLENTY OF GRUYÈRE CHEESE. THIS IS A FISHERMAN'S SOUP, SO EAT IT WITH GUSTO.

INGREDIENTS (for 4)

1kg/2lb 4oz small Mediterranean fish, chosen from wrasse, rockfish, gurnard, rascasse, conger eel, John Dory, monkfish or dorade
100ml/3½fl oz/½ cup olive oil
150g/5oz onion, coarsely chopped
1 whole head garlic, split in half
100g/3½oz fennel, coarsely chopped
1 Bouquet Garni (page 18)
1 teaspoon saffron strands
3 tablespoons Cognac
3 tablespoons white wine
200g/7oz ripe tomatoes, chopped
1 litre/1¾ pints/4½ cups cold water
few stalks of basil
few stalks of parsley
sea salt and freshly ground black pepper

TO GARNISH:

1 x quantity Rouille (page 21)
1 small, thin baguette loaf
oil for frying (optional)
150g/5oz Gruyère cheese, grated

1 First, prepare the fish. Remove and discard the eyes and gills (these will make the fish taste bitter) but leave the bones, then chop into small pieces.

2 In a large saucepan, heat one-third of the oil, then sauté the onion, garlic, fennel, Bouquet Garni and saffron.

3 Meanwhile, in a large frying pan, heat the remaining oil and fry the fish pieces for about 7 minutes or until they are golden. Drain through a colander and discard the oil.

4 Add the fish to the saucepan, then deglaze with the Cognac. When the Cognac has reduced, add the wine and simmer briskly until the liquid has reduced to about one tablespoon.

5 Add the tomatoes, water, basil and parsley stalks. Bring to the boil then simmer for 25 minutes, skimming off any froth with a ladle every 5 minutes.

6 Strain the contents of the pan through a colander set over a large bowl. Reserve the strained liquor. Reserve the fish and vegetables in the colander.

7 Discard the garlic and Bouquet Garni. Purée the fish and vegetables through a food processor, thinning the purée with a little of the reserved liquor until smooth.

8 With the back of a ladle rub the purée through a fine sieve set over a saucepan, then stir in the reserved liquor. Check the seasoning. Set aside while you prepare the garnish of Rouille (page 21) and croûtons.

9 Have ready the Rouille. For the croûtons, slice the baguette very thinly and either fry in hot oil, turning once until golden brown and crisp, or place in an oven preheated to about 180°C/350°F/Gas Mark 4 and toast for around 15-20 minutes.

10 Just before serving, reheat the soup gently while you spread the croûtons with Rouille. Ladle the soup into large, warmed bowls, float the croûtons on top and sprinkle over the grated Gruyère.

Red mullet soup

FRESH RED MULLET (ROUGET) IS BECOMING INCREASINGLY POPULAR IN THE UK, NOT ONLY FOR ITS VIBRANT SKIN COLOUR, BUT ALSO FOR ITS FINE FLAVOUR AND TENDER, FLAKY TEXTURE. IT MAKES A GOOD SOUP AND, IN THE RESTAURANT, WE SERVE IT WITH LITTLE TORTELLINI STUFFED WITH A FILLING MADE FROM THE FISH LIVER. BUY WHOLE FISH, UNGUTTED AND DESCALED, AND ASK YOUR FISHMONGER TO FILLET THEM, SAVING THE HEADS AND BONES FOR THE BASE OF THE SOUP.

INGREDIENTS (for 4)

1 litre/1¾ pints/4½ cups Fish Stock (page 14)
4 small red mullets, each weighing about 125g/4oz, prepared into fillets but with heads and bones reserved
2 pinches of saffron strands
1 pinch of cayenne pepper
a little olive oil, for sautéeing
2 shallots, sliced
½ head celery, roughly chopped
1 medium bulb fennel, roughly chopped
2 cloves garlic, unpeeled
100g/3½oz tomatoes, chopped
1 teaspoon Pernod
a little lemon juice
sea salt and freshly ground white pepper

TO GARNISH:

1 small carrot, cut into fine julienne strips
1 small courgette, cut into fine julienne strips

1 Have ready the Fish Stock and set aside. Wash the red mullet fillets, heads and bones in cold water. Pat dry with kitchen paper towels then remove any pin bones with tweezers.

2 Sprinkle the fillets with the saffron and cayenne, cover with cling film and set aside in a cool place or refrigerator to marinate for about 2 hours.

3 Sauté the fish heads and bones with a little of the oil in a large saucepan, for about 5 minutes or until golden brown.

4 Add the vegetables and tomato and cook for a further 5 minutes or so. Stir in the Pernod and cook until it has evaporated.

5 Pour in the Fish Stock so as to cover the contents of the pan. Bring slowly to the boil. Turn down to a gentle simmer and cook for 30 minutes.

6 Transfer the contents of the pan to a food processor or liquidizer and blend until smooth. Strain first through a fine sieve, then through a colander lined with wet muslin or clean fine cloth; this thorough straining will give you a good clear soup. Set aside.

7 Blanch the julienne of carrot and courgette in lightly salted boiling water, then drain and chill in ice-cold water. Drain again and set aside.

8 When you are almost ready to serve, pan fry the fillets of red mullet, skin-side down, in a little more olive oil for about 2 minutes or until golden brown; then flip over carefully and cook the other side for just 30 seconds.

9 Return the soup to the pan and reheat until just boiling. Season with lemon juice, salt and pepper. Place the fried fillets of red mullet in the bottom of each soup plate and slowly pour over the hot, clear soup. Garnish with the julienne of carrot and courgette and serve immediately.

Red mullet soup

Pumpkin soup with roasted scallops

WHEN PUMPKINS ARE IN SEASON THIS IS A GLORIOUS SOUP TO MAKE FOR A SMALL CROWD. EVEN WHEN THEY ARE NOT AROUND IN GREENGROCERS' SHOPS, PUMPKINS CAN OFTEN BE TRACKED DOWN IN ETHNIC FOOD STORES OR IN WEST INDIAN MARKETS. IDEALLY, MAKE THIS SOUP WITH FISH STOCK, WHICH GOES WELL WITH THE GARNISH OF SCALLOPS. OTHERWISE CHICKEN STOCK (PAGE 18) OR VEGETABLE NAGE (PAGE 13) WILL BE FINE.

1 Have ready the Fish Stock and set aside. Quarter the pumpkin, peel it and remove all the seeds. Chop the flesh into 1cm/½in dice.

2 In a large saucepan, heat half the oil then stir in the diced pumpkin, stirring well to coat. Cover and sweat the flesh gently for about 10–12 minutes or until it starts to soften and takes on a golden colour.

3 Pour in the Fish Stock, bring to the boil then simmer for a further 15 minutes, stirring occasionally. Add the Parmesan and cook for a further 5 minutes. Remove from the heat.

4 In a food processor or liquidizer, blend the contents of the pan to a purée. Pass the purée through a fine sieve set over the pan, rubbing with the back of a ladle or wooden spoon until very smooth and silky. If it looks a little thick, add more stock or water to thin it down a little. Taste and adjust seasoning.

5 Blanch the spinach quickly in a little boiling water then drain well, pressing the leaves dry in a clean tea towel.

6 Heat the remaining oil in a large, heavy-based frying pan and 'roast' the scallops for about 2 minutes on each side or until they have plenty of colour. Remove from the pan and split each scallop in half with a sharp knife.

7 Divide the scallops and spinach leaves between each soup bowl. Reheat the soup, gradually stirring in the butter and cream, and taste once again for seasoning.

8 When the soup is on the point of boiling, ladle it over the scallops and spinach, then sprinkle over the chervil. Serve immediately.

INGREDIENTS (for 8)

1 litre/1¾ pints/4½ cups Fish Stock (page 14)
1 x 2.5kg/5½lb pumpkin
50ml/2fl oz/¼ cup olive oil
85g/3oz Parmesan cheese, freshly grated
100g/3½oz baby spinach leaves
8 scallops, shelled, trimmed and washed (below)
25g/1oz/¼ stick butter
100ml/3½fl oz/½ cup double cream
1 tablespoon chopped chervil
sea salt and freshly ground black pepper

OPENING A SCALLOP

HOLD THE SCALLOP FIRMLY WRAPPED IN A THICK TEA TOWEL TO PREVENT SLIPPING. USING A SHORT, FIRM-BLADED KNIFE, INSERT THE POINT BETWEEN THE TWO SHELLS AND PRISE THEM APART. DISCARD THE TOP SHELL. SLIDE THE KNIFE BENEATH THE MUSCLE TO SEVER IT AND DISCARD THE BOTTOM SHELL. PULL AWAY THE FRILLY MEMBRANE AND THE BLACK INTESTINE. DISCARD THE ORANGE-PINK CORAL OR USE THIS TO MAKE CORAL POWDER (PAGE 56). WASH THE SCALLOP MEAT, COVER WITH CLING FILM AND CHILL UNTIL REQUIRED.

Mussel soup with red peppers

With the increasing number of mussel beds now around the coasts of Europe, it is possible to buy fresh mussels almost all year round. This is a really delicious light, clear soup to serve hot in the chilly months of winter or chilled in the warmer, carefree days of summer.

INGREDIENTS (for 4-6)

1.5 litres/2¾ pints/6½ cups Fish Stock (page 14)
2kg/4½lb fresh mussels, shells tightly closed
200ml/7fl oz/⅞ cup dry white wine
1 Bouquet Garni (page 18)
3 tablespoons olive oil
2 shallots, coarsely chopped
1 celery stick, chopped
1 leek, white only, sliced
2 cloves garlic, unpeeled and crushed
1 large potato, weighing about 250g/8oz, peeled and chopped
4 tomatoes, chopped
good pinch of saffron
1 tablespoon Pernod
100ml/3½fl oz/½ cup double cream
sea salt and freshly ground black pepper

TO GARNISH:

100g/3½oz red pepper, finely diced
100g/3½oz yellow pepper, finely diced

1 Have ready the Fish Stock and set aside.

2 Wash the mussels three times in cold water, scrubbing if necessary to remove any beards. Heat a large pan and, when hot, add all the mussels, two-thirds of the wine and the Bouquet Garni. Cover and give the pan a good shake. Cook, turning the mussels once, until their shells have opened – about 5 minutes. Discard any that remain closed.

3 Remove from the heat and drain through a colander, reserving the liquor (you should have about 500ml/18fl oz/2 cups). Pick the mussels from the shells. Set aside about one-third of the mussels for the garnish and discard the shells.

4 In another large saucepan, heat the oil and sweat the shallots, celery, leek, garlic and potato until lightly coloured, about 5-7 minutes.

5 Add the mussels not being used for the garnish, together with the tomatoes, and cook for a further 4 minutes. Deglaze with the remaining wine, cooking until reduced by half.

6 Stir in the saffron, Pernod, 1.4 litres/2½ pints/6 cups of the Fish Stock and the reserved mussel liquor. Bring to the boil then turn down the heat and simmer for 15-18 minutes.

7 In a food processor or liquidizer, blend the ingredients to a purée, then rub through a fine sieve with the back of a ladle. Set aside.

8 For the garnish, cook the diced peppers in a little salted boiling water for about 2 minutes then drain. Reheat the reserved mussels in the remaining Fish Stock and drain.

9 Reheat the soup until it is just approaching the boil, then stir in the cream and adjust the seasoning. Place the reserved whole mussels and diced peppers in the bottom of warmed soup bowls. Pour over the soup and serve immediately.

Lobster soup with

Lobster soup with summer vegetables

I LIKE TO SPEND MY HOLIDAYS IN THE SOUTH OF FRANCE, NOT ONLY TO UNWIND BUT ALSO TO GAIN INSPIRATION FROM THE LOCAL CUISINE. THIS IS A VERY DIFFERENT STYLE OF LOBSTER BISQUE – ALMOST A MAIN MEAL – WHICH I FIRST SAW IN THE FRENCH MEDITERRANEAN. IT IS BEST SERVED CHILLED, IDEALLY ON A SUMMER'S DAY. AS YOU WILL NEED TO BUY FOUR LOBSTERS, IT IS PROBABLY BEST-SUITED TO A SPECIAL MEAL. IF YOU PREFER TO BUY YOUR LOBSTERS READY COOKED, THEY WILL NOT NEED TO BE COOKED IN THE COURT-BOUILLON (STEP 4).

INGREDIENTS (for 4)

1 litre/1¾ pints/4½ cups Lobster Stock, made by following the recipe for Langoustine Stock (page 15) and substituting lobster shells
about 3 litres/5 pints Court-bouillon (page 16)
100ml/3½fl oz/½ cup Basic Salad Vinaigrette (page 19)
100ml/3½fl oz/½ cup double cream
1 teaspoon each of chopped tarragon and basil
100g/3½oz baby carrots, lightly scraped
100g/3½oz baby leeks, outer leaves peeled
100g/3½oz/¾ cup broad beans, podded (thawed if frozen)
100g/3½oz/½ cup petits pois (thawed if frozen)
100g/3½oz baby onions, peeled
50g/2oz fresh girolles, lightly peeled
a little butter, for sautéeing
squeeze of lemon juice
4 live baby lobsters, each weighing 350-500g/12-16oz
sea salt and freshly ground black pepper

TO GARNISH:

sprigs of flat-leaf parsley and tarragon

1 Have ready the Lobster Stock, the Court-bouillon and the Basic Salad Vinaigrette. Boil down the Lobster Stock until it has reduced by two-thirds to about 350ml/12fl oz/1½ cups. Stir in the cream and the chopped herbs. Season and set aside, leaving the herbs to infuse in the cooking liquid. When cold, strain through a fine sieve and chill the soup.

2 Meanwhile, place all the vegetables, except the girolles, in a large pan of boiling salted water. Cover and blanch for 3 minutes. Drain well and toss in the Basic Salad Vinaigrette while still warm. Leave to cool.

3 Sweat the girolles in the butter for 2 minutes or so, then mix in a squeeze of lemon juice. Set aside to cool.

4 In a stockpot or large saucepan, bring the Court-bouillon to the boil. Add the lobsters and cook them for 5-6 minutes. Leave to cool in the liquor. When you are ready to serve, remove the lobsters from the Court-bouillon.

5 Cut the lobsters in half and scoop out the flesh from the body and claws, preferably in whole pieces.

6 Divide the lightly chilled lobster soup between large, wide soup bowls. Slice the lobster meat and place in a ring in the centre of each bowl. Garnish round the outside with the reserved vegetables and sprigs of parsley and tarragon.

summer vegetables

Oyster and scallop soup

Sometimes, instead of submerging ingredients in soup, I like to lift them up on the plate – here with a mound of homemade Tagliatelle – so they retain their separate flavours, with the liquor served as a light sauce. In the Aubergine, we serve this soup with a garnish of caviar.

INGREDIENTS (for 4)

150ml/¼ pint/⅔ cup Fish Stock plus a little extra for poaching (page 14)

250ml/9fl oz/1 cup Fish Velouté (page 14)

100g/3½oz homemade Tagliatelle (page 29) or fresh ready-made

½ cucumber, peeled

4 large oysters, removed from their shells, juices reserved (page 36)

2 large scallops, shelled, trimmed and washed (page 40)

juice of ½ lemon

2 teaspoons finely chopped chives

knob of butter

sea salt and freshly ground black pepper

1 Have ready the Fish Stock, the Fish Velouté and the homemade Tagliatelle if using, and set aside.

2 Cut the cucumber into 5cm/2in lengths. Stand each piece upright and slice off the four edges around the seeds. Discard the square seed-block in the centre. Cut each slice into thin julienne strips and set aside.

3 Poach the cucumber in a little Fish Stock – just enough to cover – for about 3 minutes. Drain and keep warm.

4 In a large, heavy-based saucepan, bring the remaining Fish Stock and the Fish Velouté to the boil. Add the reserved oyster juice. Turn down to a very gentle simmer and poach the oysters for about 30 seconds. Add the scallops and cook for a further 30 seconds. Add the lemon juice, the chives and seasoning to taste; set aside in a warm place.

5 Cook the homemade Tagliatelle in a little boiling water with the butter added until just tender, about 2-3 minutes. If you are using fresh ready-made pasta, follow the pack instructions. Drain, and lift up a quarter of the pasta onto a fork and roll into a spiral.

6 Push the spiral off the fork into the centre of a large, warmed soup bowl, then put some cucumber strips on top. Repeat with the other bowls.

7 Using a slotted spoon, remove the oysters and scallops from their poaching liquid and arrange them neatly around the pasta. Bring the soup back to the boil, spoon it over the shellfish and serve immediately.

Oyster and scallop soup

Cucumber gazpacho

ONE OF OUR MOST POPULAR SOUPS. WE SERVE THIS CHILLED, AS AN *AMUSE-GUEULE*, IN SMALL *DEMITASSE* CUPS BEFORE THE START OF A MEAL. IT IS ALSO GOOD SERVED IN LARGER PORTIONS ACCOMPANIED BY A LITTLE CAVIAR, PRAWNS OR COOKED, FLAKED CRAB. THE MAIN FLAVOUR OF THE CUCUMBER IS ACCENTUATED BY THE INCLUSION OF HORSERADISH. FRESH HORSERADISH CAN BE FOUND IN SOME SPECIALITY GREENGROCERS OR YOU CAN GROW YOUR OWN. YOU WILL NEED TO START MAKING THIS SOUP A DAY AHEAD.

INGREDIENTS (for 6-8)

300ml/½ pint/1¼ cups Vegetable Nage (page 13)
4 whole cucumbers
200ml/7fl oz/⅞ cup double cream
100g/3½oz grated fresh horseradish or about 3 tablespoons horseradish relish
2 tablespoons each of chopped basil, tarragon, chervil and chives
150g/5oz/½ cup mascarpone cheese
squeeze of lemon juice
2 tablespoons creamed horseradish
sea salt and freshly ground black pepper

1 Have ready the Vegetable Nage and set aside.

2 Peel the cucumbers, cut in half lengthways and scoop out the seeds with a teaspoon. Chop half of the cucumber into fine dice for the garnish; cover and set aside in the refrigerator.

3 Cut the remaining cucumber half into thin slices, then marinate for 24 hours in a large bowl with the Vegetable Nage, cream, fresh horseradish or horseradish relish and half the herbs.

4 In a food processor or liquidizer, purée the mixture until smooth (you may have to do this in two batches), then pass the purée through a fine sieve set over a large bowl, rubbing with the back of a ladle or wooden spoon.

5 Whisk about a cupful of the purée into the mascarpone until it becomes smooth, then blend with the rest of the cucumber purée. Adjust the seasoning, adding a good squeeze of lemon juice. Stir in the creamed horseradish. Chill the soup for at least 6-8 hours before eating.

6 Serve the soup garnished with the reserved diced cucumber and the remaining herbs.

Velouté of artichokes with foie gras

THE NOBLE GLOBE ARTICHOKE IS EXTREMELY VERSATILE. IN PARIS I ATE ARTICHOKES BRAISED WITH PHEASANT LEGS, AND THEY ARE PARTICULARLY GOOD SERVED WITH A SAUTÉ OF MUSHROOMS. HERE I HAVE TAKEN A RUSTIC SOUP BASE AND ADDED THE SOPHISTICATION OF FOIE GRAS AND RAVIOLI OF CÈPES. IF YOU DON'T FEEL LIKE MAKING RAVIOLI (STEPS 5-6) THEN SIMPLY GARNISH WITH SLICED, SAUTÉED MUSHROOMS. VEGETARIANS CAN USE VEGETABLE NAGE INSTEAD OF CHICKEN STOCK, AND OMIT THE FOIE GRAS.

INGREDIENTS (for 6)

800ml/1 pint 6fl oz/3½ cups Chicken Stock (page 18) or Vegetable Nage (page 13)
6 large globe artichokes
juice of ½ lemon
50ml/2fl oz/¼ cup olive oil
100g/3½oz shallots, finely sliced
1 Bouquet Garni (page 18)
2 tablespoons white wine
20g/¾oz foie gras, fresh or canned
100ml/3½fl oz/½ cup double cream
sea salt and freshly ground black pepper

FOR THE RAVIOLI:

150g/5oz homemade Pasta Dough (page 27)
150g/5oz fresh cèpes or a mixture of brown mushrooms, shiitakes and oyster mushrooms
50g/2oz/½ stick butter plus a knob for reheating
2 teaspoons chopped chervil
1 egg yolk beaten with a pinch of salt and 2 teaspoons water

1 Have ready the Chicken Stock or Vegetable Nage and set aside.

2 Snap off the stalks and pull all the leaves from the artichokes, trimming down to the chokes and hearts. Remove and discard the hairy chokes then slice the hearts. Drop the slices into a bowl of cold water with the lemon juice added to stop them from turning brown. When you are ready to sauté the artichokes, drain them well and pat dry.

3 In a large saucepan, heat the oil and gently sauté the artichoke slices and shallots, together with the Bouquet Garni, until the vegetables are golden and begin to caramelize – about 8–10 minutes.

4 Deglaze the pan with the white wine and, when it has evaporated, pour in the Chicken Stock or Vegetable Nage. Bring to the boil, then simmer for about 20 minutes. Remove and discard the Bouquet Garni. In a food processor or liquidizer, blend the mixture to a purée, then rub it though a fine sieve with the back of a ladle; set aside to cool.

5 Make the ravioli. Cut 6 slices of cèpes, or mushrooms of your choice, for the garnish and finely chop the remainder. Melt the butter in a frying pan, sauté the slices quickly, remove from the pan and reserve. Add the chopped cèpes or mushrooms to the pan and sauté until softened, about 5 minutes. Season well, mix in the chervil, drain, cool and chill. Shape the mixture into 6 balls and set aside.

6 Roll out the pasta to the thinnest setting on a pasta machine. To make the ravioli, cut out twelve 9cm/3½in circles and enclose a ball of filling in each pair of circles. Use the beaten egg wash to ensure the edges are well sealed. (For full method see page 29.) Blanch and refresh in iced water (page 28).

7 To serve, reheat the soup and stir in the foie gras and cream until smooth. Check the seasoning.

8 Reheat the ravioli in a pan with a little water and the knob of butter. Pour the soup into warmed bowls, place a ravioli in the centre of each and garnish with the sliced cèpes or mushrooms.

Tomato consommé with

Tomato consommé with little basil ravioli

WHEN TOMATOES ARE RIPE, FULL-FLAVOURED AND PLENTIFUL, WE SERVE THIS LIGHT, PRETTY SOUP HOT WITH TINY BASIL-FLAVOURED RAVIOLI FLOATING IN THE CLEAR, BRIGHT LIQUID. WE THEN GARNISH WITH JULIENNE OF *TROMPETTES DES MORTS* MUSHROOMS AND TOMATO CONCASSE. YOU CAN ALSO SERVE THIS CONSOMMÉ CHILLED, OMITTING THE RAVIOLI, AND GARNISHED WITH FINELY DICED MOZZARELLA. I'LL EXPLAIN HOW TO MAKE THE DAINTY RAVIOLI ANYWAY (STEPS 7-8), BECAUSE THEY ARE A GOOD USE OF LEFTOVER PASTA DOUGH.

INGREDIENTS (for 6)

2 large shallots, finely chopped
50ml/2fl oz/¼ cup olive oil plus extra to sauté the mushrooms
1kg/2lb 4oz dark red, almost over-ripe, tomatoes, coarsely chopped
2 cloves garlic, thinly sliced
1 teaspoon each sea salt and sugar
1 teaspoon each chopped basil, tarragon and chervil
1 litre/1¾ pints/4½ cups cold water
stalks of basil and tarragon
4 egg whites
6 white peppercorns
6 black peppercorns

FOR THE RAVIOLI (OPTIONAL):

100g/3½oz homemade Pasta Dough (page 27)
50g/2oz basil leaves
a little olive oil, to moisten
1 egg yolk beaten with a pinch of salt and 2 teaspoons water

TO GARNISH:

50g/2oz/¾ cup trompettes des morts *or oyster mushrooms, cut into fine julienne strips*
100g/3½oz/½ cup Tomato Concasse (page 97)
1 tablespoon small whole basil, tarragon and chervil leaves

1 In a large, heavy-based saucepan, sweat the shallots in the oil over a very low heat for about 5-6 minutes until they just begin to colour.

2 Add 800g/1lb 12oz of the tomatoes and cook for a further 10 minutes. Stir in the garlic, salt, sugar and chopped herbs.

3 Pour in the water and bring to the boil. Skim to clear the surface using a large spoon or ladle, then simmer gently for about 15 minutes.

4 Line a colander with a large piece of wet muslin or a clean, old tea towel and stand it over a large pan. Pour the liquid through the colander, pushing down on the vegetables with the back of a ladle to extract as much juice as possible. Discard the vegetables and chill the liquor as quickly as possible by standing the pan in a sink of iced water. Wash the cloth to reuse later.

5 Liquidize the remaining tomatoes with the basil and tarragon stalks, egg whites and peppercorns in a food processor, then add to the pan containing the cold tomato liquor.

6 To clarify the liquor, bring it slowly to the boil, then simmer for about 15 minutes until the stock becomes clear. Line the colander again with the wet muslin or tea towel over a large bowl or container; carefully ladle through the stock. Cool down the consommé again as quickly as possible.

7 If making the basil ravioli for the hot version, have ready the homemade Pasta Dough. Purée the basil leaves with just a touch of olive oil to a fine paste, using a food processor or a pestle and mortar. Spoon this paste into a piping bag fitted with a plain 5mm/¼in nozzle. Place the bag in the refrigerator to chill.

▶

little basil ravioli

8 Roll out the Pasta Dough as thinly as possible (steps 2-3, page 27). Pipe dots of the basil paste – to the size of chocolate drops – at 3cm/1¼in intervals, so that the dots form neat, lengthways rows down one half of the pasta sheet. Allow about 8 ravioli per portion.

9 Brush in between the dots carefully with the beaten egg wash. Fold over the unglazed half of the sheet and press together the rows of ravioli with your fingers around the dots of filling. Using the end of a plain 2cm/¾in piping nozzle as a cutter, cut out as many ravioli as you can.

10 Bring a saucepan of water to the boil and blanch the ravioli for just 10 seconds. Plunge into cold water to arrest their cooking, then drain and set aside.

11 Heat the remaining oil in a frying pan and sauté the mushrooms until softened. Pat dry with kitchen paper towels.

12 To serve hot, reheat the consommé and add the ravioli if you have made them. Spoon into warmed soup bowls and garnish with the julienne of mushrooms, Tomato Concasse and herbs.

13 To serve chilled, without the ravioli, chill the sautéed mushrooms briefly, and serve as a garnish together with the Tomato Concasse and the herbs.

Broccoli soup with little goat's cheese ravioli

The soup ingredients may look disappointingly bland – broccoli, water, salt and a little cream – but it is the technique that makes this vibrant green soup so sublime; and it is reassuringly simple. For a garnish, make either a host of baby ravioli filled with dots of creamed goat's cheese (steps 6-9 and 11) or, for a simpler garnish, make quenelles (page 173) from the goat's cheese mixture and float these on top of the hot soup. Either way, the pale garnish looks good against the colourful soup.

INGREDIENTS (for 6)

2kg/4½lb broccoli heads
1.5 litres/2¼ pints/6½ cups cold water
4 teaspoons sea salt
120ml/4fl oz/½ cup 1 tablespoon double cream
freshly ground black pepper

FOR THE RAVIOLI:

150g/5oz homemade Pasta Dough (page 27)
75g/3oz soft goat's cheese, e.g. crottin
2 tablespoons mascarpone cheese
1 egg yolk beaten with a pinch of salt and 2 teaspoons water

1 Trim the florets from the broccoli heads. This is very important – you should have virtually no stalks attached, just the last 2cm/¾in or so. The finished weight of florets should be around 800g/1lb 12oz.

2 Bring the water to a rolling boil with the salt. Add the florets and cook for 10 minutes.

3 Drain, but reserve the water. This is vital! Return the florets to the pan and heat for 2-3 minutes to dry them out, shaking the pan frequently. Again this is an important stage.

4 Blend the florets in a food processor or liquidizer, adding a ladleful of the reserved cooking water at a time, and stopping the machine once or twice to scrape down the sides. Continue until you have a really silky, smooth, startlingly bright green purée. You may find this easiest to do in two or even three batches. The purée should be the texture of soft, runny butter with a glossy sheen and without even the tiniest lump.

5 Thin with a little more of the reserved water then pass the purée through a fine sieve. Set aside to cool, together with the remainder of the reserved water.

6 If making the ravioli, have ready the homemade Pasta Dough and roll it out thinly (Ravioli, steps 1-2, page 29).

7 Beat the goat's cheese and mascarpone together until smoothly blended, then spoon into a piping bag fitted with a plain 5mm/¼in nozzle. Pipe small dots over half the pasta at intervals of about 2.5cm/1in. Don't make the dots too large – they should be the size of large chocolate drops.

8 Using a thin pastry- or paint brush, brush in between with the beaten egg wash then fold the other half of the dough over, allowing it to fall over the dots of creamed goat's cheese mixture.

9 Using the end of a 2cm/¾in plain piping nozzle as a cutter, cut out the tiny ravioli. The action of pressing down with the nozzle seals the pasta layers together. Using a palette knife, scoop up the ravioli and set aside.

10 Just prior to serving, bring the broccoli purée to the boil and slowly stir in about three-quarters of the reserved cooking liquid, then mix in the cream. Check the seasoning and consistency. If you want a thinner soup, add more of the reserved water. Keep the soup hot.

11 Plunge the ravioli into a pan of rapidly boiling salted water and simmer them for just 20 seconds. With a slotted spoon, remove the ravioli and place in warmed soup bowls. Ladle over the hot soup and serve immediately.

Starters

A starter is perhaps the most influential part of a meal. It is a chef's introduction to the diner of his style and it sets the scene of what is to follow. If it is exciting, then you are intrigued. If it is brilliant, then you know that nine times out of ten the main course will be even better.

My personal favourites as starters are light fish or vegetable terrines (or, as I prefer to call them, mosaics). Take the Salad of Sautéed Langoustine and Candied Aubergine (page 54): this is a clever dish – a blissfully happy marriage of plump, roasted langoustines and full-flavoured fresh Tomato Concasse (page 97), topped with wafer-thin aubergine slices sprinkled with sugar and baked to a light crispness.

My summer-style mosaics may look dauntingly difficult to make, but rest assured – they are easy! It is simply a question of assembling some best-quality ingredients combined with the basic building block of a good stock. I love making mosaics and burst with excitement to turn them out and cut the first slice quickly. What will it look like? What picture will it create on the plate?

Salad of sautéed langoustine and candied aubergine

THIS DISH CONTAINS TWO CLASSIC EXAMPLES OF MY ORIGINAL STYLE OF COOKING: THE SPECTACULAR PINK COATING OF THE FRESH PAN-FRIED LANGOUSTINES (DUBLIN BAY PRAWNS), WHICH COMES FROM THE SMALL GREEN SACS FOUND IN THE HEADS OF LIVE LOBSTERS AND WHICH WE CALL THE 'CORAL', AND THE TOPPING OF CRISP CANDIED AUBERGINE SLICES. THESE ARE SERVED ON A RING OF FRESH PROVENÇAL SAUCE SET AROUND A DELICATE MOUND OF MIXED SALAD LEAVES. FULL OF FLAVOUR AND A TREAT TO THE EYE, THE LANGOUSTINE CAN BE PREPARED WITHOUT THE COATING IF NECESSARY.

INGREDIENTS (for 2)

about 2 tablespoons Basic Salad Vinaigrette (page 19)
16 Candied Aubergine Slices (page 180)
about 100g/3½oz Mixed Salad Leaves (below)
2 sprigs chervil
16 fresh langoustines, peeled and de-veined
2 teaspoons fresh lobster 'coral' (tomalley)
2 tablespoons olive oil

FOR THE PROVENÇAL SAUCE:

½ tomato, skinned and seeded
1 teaspoon finely diced, pitted black olives
½ teaspoon each of chopped basil and tarragon
squeeze of lemon juice
sea salt and freshly ground black pepper

1 Have ready the Basic Salad Vinaigrette and set aside. Also have ready the Candied Aubergines and keep warm.

2 Prepare the Mixed Salad Leaves. Pick off the leaves of chervil and incorporate these into the salad; set aside.

3 To make the Provençal sauce, chop the skinned tomato into fine dice and mix with the olives, basil, tarragon, lemon juice and seasoning. Transfer to a small saucepan and heat until just warm but not hot.

4 Toss the langoustines in the lobster 'coral'.

5 Heat the oil until hot and fry the langoustines for about 2 minutes, stirring until lightly cooked and bright pink. Drain on kitchen paper towels.

6 Dress the Mixed Salad Leaves with the Basic Salad Vinaigrette and arrange in mounds in the centre of each plate. Spoon the warm Provençal sauce around the salad, then place eight langoustines on each plate, arranging them in a ring on top of the sauce. Balance a Candied Aubergine Slice on top of each langoustine and serve immediately.

MIXED SALAD LEAVES

I LIKE TO PAY PARTICULAR ATTENTION TO OUR GREEN SALAD IN THE AUBERGINE. JUST ANY OLD LEAF SIMPLY WON'T DO. WE USE A MIXTURE OF ROCKET, FRISÉE, LOLLO ROSSO AND OAK LEAF, PICKING OFF AND USING ONLY THE YOUNG TENDER TIPS. THESE ARE GENTLY WASHED, SPUN IN A SALAD SPINNER UNTIL DRY, THEN PLACED IN A BOWL, COVERED WITH CLING FILM AND KEPT IN THE REFRIGERATOR UNTIL REQUIRED.

Roasted scallops with fennel and a ginger cream

The best scallops are those that are hand picked by divers rather than dredged, as they are free from grit. Make sure they are tightly closed when you buy them, as this shows they are really fresh. Although you don't need the coral for this recipe, don't waste it as it can be dried and ground into a fine powder and used as a flavouring for risottos and sauces (page 56).

INGREDIENTS (for 4)

450ml/¾ pint/2 cups Fish Velouté (page 14)
4 tablespoons Fish Stock (page 14)
100g/3½oz grated fresh root ginger
2 medium bulbs of fennel, sliced
100g/3½oz shallots, sliced
6 tablespoons olive oil
2 tablespoons white wine
80ml/3fl oz/⅓ cup double cream
squeeze of lemon juice
6 prepared scallops, each weighing about 25g/1oz, halved lengthways (page 40)
sea salt

1 Have ready the Fish Velouté and the Fish Stock. Add the ginger to the Fish Velouté and allow to infuse for a few minutes. Strain it out, returning the Fish Velouté to a saucepan; set aside.

2 Put the fennel, shallots and half the oil in a frying pan, heat until sizzling then cover and lower the heat. Allow the vegetables to sweat gently for about 12 minutes until softened; shake the pan occasionally and do not allow the vegetables to colour.

3 Stir in the wine, raise the heat slightly and cook, uncovered, until it has evaporated. Stir in the Fish Stock and boil until it has reduced by about half and looks syrupy.

4 Stir in the cream and cook for a further 3-4 minutes. Transfer the mixture to a food processor or a liquidizer and blend to a soft purée. Return to the pan to keep warm and season to taste with lemon juice and salt.

5 Start gently reheating the gingered Fish Velouté.

6 In a frying pan, heat the remaining oil until almost smoking and add the scallops, placing them in a clockwise direction. Cook for 3 minutes in total, turning once only, again in a clockwise direction; this ensures even cooking. Season well.

7 To serve, spoon the fennel purée in a neat round in the centre of each warmed soup plate. Place three scallop halves onto each circle of purée.

8 When the gingered Fish Velouté just approaches the boil, taste for seasoning, adding more lemon juice and salt if necessary. Froth up with a Bamix (see page 189 for supplier) or a hand-held electric multi-blender until you have a good foam, then spoon the sauce around the fennel purée. Serve immediately.

▶

To make scallop coral powder

INSTEAD OF THROWING AWAY SCALLOP CORALS, DRY THEM THEN GRIND THEM DOWN TO A FINE POWDER FOR FLAVOURING. USE AS REQUIRED, A TABLESPOON OR SO AT A TIME, STIRRING INTO SAUCES OR RISOTTOS FOR A DELICIOUS FLAVOUR AND GLORIOUS COLOUR.

1 Slice each coral in half and remove any dirt. Place on a baking sheet lined with non-stick baking film. Set the oven to its lowest temperature, about 80-100°C/175-225°F/Gas Mark ½. If your oven has a pilot light you may prefer to use this method of heating.

2 Leave the corals in the oven for anything between 8-16 hours or until they are dark pink and quite brittle. They should snap when they are ready. If they don't snap, return them to the oven, testing at intervals, until they do snap.

3 Place the corals in a food processor a few at a time and grind to a fine powder. (This will make quite a noise!) Store in a screw-top jar.

Roasted scallops with

fennel and a ginger cream

Mille-feuille of red mullet and langoustine

SAFFRON-FLAVOURED FILLETS OF RED MULLET AND LANGOUSTINES ARE LAYERED IN A STUNNING 'MILLE-FEUILLE' ARRANGEMENT AND SERVED WITH A TRICKLE OF OLIVE OIL. MAKE SURE THAT THE LANGOUSTINES ARE VERY FRESH AND FIRM WHEN YOU BUY THEM.

1 Have ready the Aubergine Caviar and Vegetable Nage and set aside.
2 Shell the langoustines, then make a lengthways split in each, without cutting through completely so that you can open them up into a butterfly shape. Clean if necessary, then brush with some of the oil and season.
3 Crush the saffron strands over the red mullet fillets and rub in well. This will give them a lovely yellow colour and aromatic flavour.
4 Blanch the basil leaves briefly in boiling water then plunge them into iced water. Mix with the Vegetable Nage and purée in a food processor or liquidizer then set aside.
5 Cook the 'turned' new potatoes in boiling salted water for about 7 minutes or until just tender. Drain and keep in a warm place.
6 Just prior to serving, heat through the Aubergine Caviar, check the seasoning and keep warm.
7 Heat two-thirds of the remaining oil in a heavy-based frying pan and lightly sauté the mullet and langoustines. For the mullet, allow 2 minutes on the skin side and 30 seconds on the flesh side. For the langoustines, allow 1 minute on each side. Remove from the pan and drain.
8 Divide the Aubergine Caviar between each warmed plate in a mound in the centre and stack the mullet and then the langoustine on top. Pour a little of the basil sauce around each mound, arrange six potatoes on the sauce and garnish each potato with a Candied Aubergine Slice. Finish by trickling over the last of the oil.

INGREDIENTS (for 2)

½ x quantity Aubergine Caviar (page 101)
6 medium to large langoustines
100ml/3½fl oz/½ cup olive oil
pinch of saffron strands
2 red mullets, each weighing about 100g/3½oz, filleted into four
sea salt and freshly ground black pepper

TO GARNISH:

3 tablespoons Vegetable Nage (page 13)
30g/1oz/½ cup basil leaves
12 baby new potatoes, 'turned' into barrel shapes
12 Candied Aubergine Slices (page 180)

Mille-feuille of red mullet and langoustine

Beignets of oysters with sauce aigre-doux

OYSTERS, FRESH FROM THE SHELL, MAY BE THE FOOD OF THE GODS BUT THEY ARE ALSO DIVINE SERVED HOT AS BEIGNETS, OR FRITTERS, IN A LIGHT, CRISP BATTER. THE BATTER IS BEST MADE WITH FRESH YEAST, AVAILABLE EITHER FROM SMALL INDEPENDENT BAKERIES OR HEALTH FOOD SHOPS. DRIED, EASY-BLEND YEAST GIVES ALMOST COMPARABLE RESULTS, ALTHOUGH THE RISING MAY TAKE A LITTLE LONGER.

1 To make the batter using fresh yeast, cream it with a little of the milk until it forms a paste. Using a balloon whisk, beat in the remaining ingredients, until smooth. Alternatively, blend in a food processor. If using easy-blend yeast, stir the dried yeast straight into the flour and add a good pinch of salt. Whisk in the remaining milk and the beer, beating until smooth.

2 Cover with cling film then set the bowl in a warm place (such as an airing cupboard) and leave until risen and frothy. This will probably take about 1 hour in the case of fresh yeast but longer for easy-blend.

3 Meanwhile, make the sauce. Have ready the Vegetable Nage. Sauté the peppers, shallots and herbs in the oil for about 10 minutes until softened. Add one teaspoon of the vinegar and cook until evaporated.

4 Pour in the Noilly Prat and cook until it has reduced by two-thirds and looks syrupy. Stir in the Vegetable Nage, bring to the boil and simmer for about 15 minutes or until the vegetables are soft.

5 Discard the sprigs of herbs and the bay leaf, then purée the vegetables in a food processor or liquidizer. Rub the puréed sauce through a fine sieve with the back of a ladle. Return the sauce to the pan and boil down for a few minutes until it has a good coating consistency. Add the remaining teaspoon of vinegar. Season to taste and set aside.

6 Prepare the Mixed Salad Leaves, season and dress with Basic Salad Vinaigrette, then place in the centre of each plate.

7 Pat the oysters dry and sprinkle with a little flour. In a deep frying pan heat the oil until it reaches a temperature of about 175°C/350°F, or until a cube of day-old bread turns crisp and golden in under 30 seconds.

8 Using your fingers or a wooden skewer, dip the oysters into the batter making sure they are well coated as the batter is quite thick. Drop each one into the hot oil and fry for about 2 minutes on each side or until golden and crisp. Remove with a slotted spoon and drain on kitchen paper towels.

9 Spoon the sauce around the Mixed Salad Leaves then arrange the oyster beignets on the sauce. Scatter over the chopped herbs and serve straight away.

INGREDIENTS (for 4)

12 fresh, prepared oysters (page 36)
a little plain flour, to sprinkle
about 500ml/18fl oz/2 cups olive oil
sea salt and freshly ground black pepper

FOR THE BATTER:

5g/⅙oz fresh yeast or 1½ teaspoons dried easy-blend yeast
250ml/9fl oz/1 cup milk, warmed until tepid
150g/5oz/1 cup plain flour
good pinch of salt
1 teaspoon beer

FOR THE SAUCE AIGRE-DOUX:

200ml/7fl oz/⅞ cup Vegetable Nage (page 13)
1 medium red pepper, cored and thinly sliced
1 medium yellow pepper, cored and thinly sliced
6 large shallots, thinly sliced
1 sprig each of thyme and tarragon
½ bay leaf
50ml/2fl oz/¼ cup olive oil
2 teaspoons white wine vinegar
200ml/7fl oz/⅞ cup Noilly Prat

TO SERVE:

200g/7oz Mixed Salad Leaves (page 54)
2 teaspoons Basic Salad Vinaigrette (page 19)
1 teaspoon each of chopped chervil and tarragon

Beignets of courgette flowers with three-mustard vinaigrette

In the restaurant trade it is, I acknowledge, quite easy to order up perfectly formed fresh courgette flowers for stuffing with a light *farce*. Sometimes, you can even buy them at quality green-grocers. However, many cooks are also keen kitchen gardeners and may well have a surfeit of these pretty, trumpet-shaped, golden flowers rambling over their vegetable plot. To make these beignets, choose flowers that are newly formed as they are flatter and so better for dipping in batter. You can also eat the whole baby courgettes attached at the stalk.

INGREDIENTS (for 4)

200g/7oz Mixed Salad Leaves (page 54)
12 medium to large courgette flowers
about 500ml/18fl oz/2 cups olive oil
sea salt

FOR THE BATTER:

5g/⅙oz fresh yeast or 1½ teaspoons dried, easy-blend yeast
250ml/9fl oz/1 cup milk, warmed until tepid
150g/5oz/1 cup plain flour
good pinch of salt
1 teaspoon beer

FOR THE DRESSING:

1 x quantity Basic Salad Vinaigrette (page 19)
1½ teaspoons wholegrain mustard
1½ teaspoons Dijon mustard
1½ teaspoons honey mustard

1 To make up batter using fresh yeast, cream it with a little of the milk until it forms a paste. Using a balloon whisk, beat in the remaining ingredients until smooth. Alternatively, blend in a food processor. If using easy-blend yeast, stir the dried yeast straight into the flour and add a good pinch of salt. Whisk in the remaining milk and the beer, beating until smooth.

2 Cover with cling film then set the bowl in a warm place (such as an airing cupboard) and leave until risen and frothy. This will probably take about 1 hour in the case of fresh yeast but longer for easy-blend.

3 Meanwhile, prepare the Basic Salad Vinaigrette and beat in the mustards; set aside. Pick over the salad leaves, discarding any thick stalks and tearing leaves into small delicate pieces.

4 To prepare the courgette flowers, snap off the little courgettes. (Don't waste them! These can be used in another dish.) One by one, hold each flower gently at its stalk end. Pick out, and discard, its inner stamen.

5 When the batter is ready, in a deep frying pan heat the oil until it reaches a temperature of about 175°C/350°F, or until a cube of day-old bread turns crisp and gold in under 30 seconds.

6 Dip the flowers one at a time into the batter, coating them well and draining off the batter just before you fry. Dip and fry about 3-4 at a time and cook for about one minute on each side, or until golden and crisp. Drain on kitchen paper towels and sprinkle with salt.

7 Toss the salad with a little of the three-mustard vinaigrette and place in mounds in the centre of each dinner plate. Trickle the remainder of the dressing in circles around the salad then arrange the beignets on the sauce allowing three for each serving.

Terrine of foie gras

Terrine of foie gras with canard confit

A very special occasion terrine, ideal for Christmas when fattened ducks and fresh foie gras are more readily available. We use duck rather than goose foie gras because it is less expensive and more suitable for a terrine. Fresh foie gras generally needs to be ordered in advance from speciality butchers, although a few such shops may sometimes have it in stock. Goose fat can be bought from speciality shops, but you may have some saved from roasting a goose. For an extra special presentation, garnish each slice with chopped port wine jelly or cold chopped consommé. You will need to start this dish a day in advance.

INGREDIENTS (makes a 1kg/2lb 4oz terrine for 8-10)

4 medium to large duck legs
2 sprigs thyme
1 sprig rosemary
250g/8oz/1 cup goose or duck fat, melted
2 x 750g/1lb 10oz whole fresh duck or goose foie gras
1 tablespoon white port
1 tablespoon Armagnac
1 tablespoon Madeira
sea salt and freshly ground black pepper

1 Pluck any hairs from the duck legs then season and sprinkle with the leaves picked from the thyme and rosemary sprigs. Cover and set aside in the refrigerator for 2 hours to allow the flavours to permeate. Preheat the oven to 170°C/325°F/Gas Mark 3.

2 Place the duck legs in a small roasting pan or cast-iron casserole, then cover with the melted goose or duck fat. Wet a large sheet of greaseproof paper, and crumple it over and around the duck legs to hold them submerged under the fat.

3 Set the roasting pan or casserole over a medium heat and bring the fat to the boil. Transfer the pan carefully to the oven. Cook for 1½-2 hours or until the meat is meltingly tender and starts to fall off the bone. Remove from the heat and leave the duck to cool in the fat.

4 Meanwhile, remove the foie gras from the refrigerator about 1-2 hours before preparation, to soften, so they are easier to handle. Carefully unravel the lobes of each liver into 2 halves and, using a small sharp knife, remove the membrane and central vein, making sure you don't damage the lobes. If you like, check for any blood spots and pick these out too. This is not essential, but the terrine will look better when it is sliced. Repeat with the other foie gras.

5 Gently remould the foie gras making sure you don't overhandle them or they could turn soft. Lay the foie gras in a deep roasting pan. Season with salt and pepper and sprinkle over the port, Armagnac and Madeira. Leave to marinate for 1 hour.

▶

with canard confit

6 Preheat the oven to 190°C/375°F/Gas Mark 5. Roast the marinated foie gras for about 12 minutes or until the liver is just soft and slightly reduced in size. A word of warning: a lot of glorious, golden fat will seep out, which you need to save. Gently remove the livers and set aside.

7 Now continue with the confit: strip the duck meat from the bones then mix with a little of the soft goose or duck fat in which it was cooked along with some seasoning. This helps bind the meat together.

8 Line the base of a 1kg/2lb loaf tin with a strip of greaseproof paper. Cut the foie gras into slices about 1cm/½in thick. Layer in the tin along with the duck pieces, pouring a little of the saved foie gras fat between each layer and finishing with a layer of foie gras.

9 Cut a sheet of foil or greaseproof paper to fit the top of the tin exactly. Lay it in position. Place measuring weights or small cans on top. The pressure should be light but even. Leave the terrine in the refrigerator overnight or until set and firm enough to slice.

10 Remove the foil or paper. Melt a little of the remaining foie gras fat and spoon some of this on top of the terrine to seal it completely. Chill in the refrigerator until set.

11 To unmould the terrine, run a hot knife blade round the inside of the loaf tin and invert onto a flat board or platter. Lift away the tin and remove the lining paper. To serve, cut into 2.5cm/1in slices. Accompany the terrine with a crisp green salad and offer slices of warm brioche toast.

Poached oysters in a watercress sauce

ANOTHER SUBLIMELY SIMPLE DISH – OYSTERS POACHED IN THEIR OWN JUICES THEN SERVED WITH A WATERCRESS VELOUTÉ AND HOMEMADE TAGLIATELLE. IF YOU DON'T HAVE TIME TO MAKE YOUR OWN TAGLIATELLE, YOU CAN SUBSTITUTE FRESH READY-MADE.

INGREDIENTS (for 2)

200ml/7fl oz/⅞ cup Fish Velouté (page 14)
200g/7oz homemade Tagliatelle (page 29) or fresh ready-made
300g/10oz fresh watercress (about 6 bunches)
10 fresh oysters
3-4 tablespoons rock salt, to serve
25g/1oz/¼ stick unsalted butter
10 tiny sprigs chervil
sea salt and freshly ground black pepper

1 Make the Fish Velouté and homemade Tagliatelle, if using, and set aside.

2 Pick the thick stalks off the watercress and discard, then wash the leaves in two or three changes of cold water.

3 Bring a pan of salted water to the boil and blanch the watercress for 3-4 minutes, then drain and squeeze lightly in a cloth to dry.

4 In a food processor or liquidizer, blend the watercress to a smooth, fine purée adding a little of the Fish Velouté to loosen the mixture if necessary.

5 Bring the Fish Velouté to the boil then stir in the watercress purée. Pass this sauce through a sieve, rubbing with the back of a ladle, then set aside.

6 Blanch the homemade Tagliatelle in boiling salted water for barely 1 minute then drain. Plunge into very cold water to refresh and drain again (steps 9-10, page 28). If using ready-made, follow the pack instructions. Set aside.

7 Open the oysters (page 36), reserving their juices and tipping these into a small pan. Discard the flat shells. Scrub the rounded shells clean and pat dry. Spoon five small mounds of rock salt onto each plate and sit an oyster shell on each.

8 Reheat the Tagliatelle in a little water with the butter. Curl a little of the prepared Tagliatelle into each cleaned oyster shell. Keep warm.

9 Poach the oysters in their own juice cooking for about 2 minutes then remove them from the juice with a slotted spoon and place on the pasta.

10 Reheat the sauce until just boiling, check the seasoning and spoon over the oysters. Garnish with the chervil sprigs and serve.

Mosaic of rabbit with cabbage and cèpes

Rabbit is highly prized in France but still regarded with some disdain in Great Britain and the USA – a pity because it is a delicious, light meat that is easy to prepare and cook. This pretty terrine is one of the most popular starters at the Aubergine. Serve with a green salad and glaze each slice with a little truffle-flavoured olive oil. For the rabbit, buy a whole, small, domesticated one, ordering in advance from your butcher if necessary. You can also adapt this recipe by substituting a good-quality free-range chicken. You will need to start the mosaic a day or so in advance.

INGREDIENTS (for 8-10)

FOR THE CONFIT:

1 rabbit, weighing about 1kg/2lb
about 800g/1lb 12oz goose fat or concentrated butter
2 bay leaves
1 sprig thyme
10 whole coriander seeds
10 black peppercorns, crushed
1 star anise
2 tablespoons coarse sea salt

FOR THE TERRINE:

1.7 litres/3 pints/7½ cups Brown Chicken Stock (page 18)
about 85g/3oz/¾ stick butter
150g/5oz young cabbage leaves, finely shredded
150g/5oz mixed wild mushrooms e.g. cèpes, shiitakes or oysters, sliced
12 new potatoes, preferably long in shape, scrubbed
6 leaves gelatine or 4 teaspoons gelatine crystals
3 tablespoons chopped chives
250g/9oz pâté de foie gras, cut into long strips
sea salt and freshly ground black pepper

1 First make the rabbit confit: preheat the oven to 180°C/350°F/Gas Mark 4. Joint the rabbit by cutting off the legs and saddle; there is no need to keep the rib cage or neck, which can be discarded.

2 Place in a ovenproof casserole. Heat the goose fat to boiling point and pour it over the rabbit. Add the bay leaves, thyme, coriander seeds, peppercorns, star anise and salt.

3 Make sure the rabbit is completely submerged beneath the fat. Cut out a sheet of greaseproof paper (we call this a *cartouche*) to fit the top of the casserole exactly. Place this on top of the fat so that the meat is held beneath the fat and prevented from browning and overcooking. If you wet the paper it will be easier to mould.

4 Cook in the oven for about 1¼ hours or until the meat is very tender. Leave to cool in the fat then remove, scrape off excess fat, herbs and spices, and remove the meat from the bones in large pieces. Make sure the meat is free of fat, veins and sinews. If you like, strain the fat and store it in the refrigerator for further use. It will keep for a good few months.

5 For the terrine, boil the Brown Chicken Stock until reduced by about half to concentrate the flavour. Set 250ml/9fl oz/1 cup aside in a saucepan for the potatoes.

6 Heat half the butter in a frying pan and sauté the cabbage quickly until just wilted. Remove with a slotted spoon. Add the remaining butter and ▶

Mosaic of rabbit with cabbage and cèpes

sauté the mushrooms until cooked; drain and set aside. Season both vegetables well and leave to cool.

7 Cook the potatoes in the reserved stock until just tender – about 10 minutes. (At the restaurant, we 'turn' these before cooking, that is, we cut them into equal-size barrel shapes; but this is optional. As long as the potatoes are long, rather than round, and roughly the same size – about 5cm/2in – the terrine will look good.) Drain, set aside and cool.

8 Bring the remaining 500ml/18fl oz/2 cups of Brown Chicken Stock to boiling point. Meanwhile, if using leaf gelatine, soak the leaves in ice-cold water for at least 5 minutes or until softened, then squeeze out the water. When the stock has boiled, stir in the leaf gelatine until dissolved. If using gelatine crystals, sprinkle directly into the just-boiled stock, stirring briskly until clear. Mix the chives into the stock, then set aside to cool – preferably over ice – stirring from time to time until the mixture just starts to thicken.

9 Using a 1.1 litre/2 pint/5 cup loaf tin, pour a little of the setting jelly in the base, and sprinkle in a little of the cabbage and mushrooms. Lay pieces of rabbit lengthways down the tin, placing potatoes and strips of foie gras in between. Pour over some jelly, making sure the chives are well distributed.

10 Add further layers of cabbage and mushrooms, then jelly, rabbit, potatoes, foie gras and more jelly, pressing the food down beneath the layers of jelly. Repeat the layering process finishing with cabbage and mushrooms and leaving a space of about 2cm/¾in at the top (you will not use all the rabbit). Pour over more jelly ensuring it completely covers the food. Tap the tin lightly on the work surface to release any air bubbles. Place carefully in the refrigerator and leave overnight or until the terrine is set and firm enough to slice.

11 To turn out the terrine, dip a palette knife in boiling water and run it around the insides of the tin to loosen. Dip the base into a bowl of very hot water and count to 10. Invert the mould onto a flat board or platter and give it a good shake. The terrine should slip out, but if it does not, dip the tin again for 10 seconds and repeat the process with a hot palette knife. For neat slices, cut with an electric carving knife, or a long serrated knife.

STORING RABBIT CONFIT

AFTER MAKING THIS RECIPE YOU WILL HAVE ABOUT HALF THE QUANTITY OF RABBIT CONFIT LEFT OVER WHICH CAN BE USED TO MAKE ANOTHER TERRINE LATER. TO PREPARE THIS FOR STORAGE, PLACE IN A BOWL, REHEAT THE GOOSE FAT AND POUR OVER ENOUGH TO COVER THE COOKED MEAT. CHILL UNTIL SET THEN COVER WITH CLING FILM. THE CONFIT SHOULD KEEP FRESH FOR A GOOD MONTH, AS LONG AS THE MEAT HAS BEEN COMPLETELY COVERED IN THE FAT.

Roasted rabbit salad with chicory à la crème

PEOPLE ARE GENERALLY FAR TOO CAUTIOUS ABOUT USING RABBIT. IF IT'S USED AT ALL, IT TENDS TO BE IN A CASSEROLE, MAYBE EVEN A TERRINE. BUT HERE IS A RECIPE FOR A SALAD OF RABBIT! THE RABBIT IS SERVED WARM AND ACCOMPANIED BY SAUTÉED WILD MUSHROOMS, SALAD LEAVES AND LIGHTLY CARAMELIZED CHICORY. IF YOU FIND IT DIFFICULT TO BUY RABBIT LEGS, BUY A WHOLE RABBIT AND FREEZE THE SADDLE FOR USE LATER.

INGREDIENTS (for 4)

3 tablespoons Basic Salad Vinaigrette (page 19)
1 tablespoon olive oil
100g/3½oz/1 stick butter
4 medium to large rabbit legs
4 large heads chicory
2 teaspoons salt
2 teaspoons sugar
200ml/7fl oz/⅞ cup double cream
300g/10oz wild mushrooms
200g/7oz Mixed Salad Leaves (page 54)
few sprigs chervil
sea salt and freshly ground black pepper

1 Have ready the Basic Salad Vinaigrette and set aside.

2 Preheat the oven to 200°C/400°F/Gas Mark 6. Heat the oil in a cast-iron pan with a knob of the butter. Sauté the rabbit legs until lightly browned all over.

3 Cover the legs with a butter paper or buttered greaseproof paper then roast in the oven for about 5 minutes or until just cooked.

4 Remove from the oven and allow to rest for 5 minutes. Cut each leg in two through the joint, then remove the meat from the bones and cut it in medallions. Toss with one-third of the Basic Salad Vinaigrette; season and set aside.

5 Cut the heads of chicory into strips, from top to bottom. Heat a quarter of the remaining butter in a pan and lightly sauté the strips, sprinkling with the salt and sugar.

6 When the strips start to soften, after about 3 minutes, remove them from the pan and wipe it out with a kitchen paper towel. Return the pan to the heat and pour in the cream.

7 Bring the cream to the boil, return the chicory strips to the pan and cook for about one minute until reduced down by about half. Set aside.

8 Cook the mushrooms in the remaining butter for about 5 minutes or until just softened. Remove and toss in another third of the remaining vinaigrette.

9 Just prior to serving, prepare the Mixed Salad Leaves, dress them lightly with the last of the Basic Salad Vinaigrette and place in a mound in the centre of each plate. Arrange the chicory strips around the salad. Spoon the mushrooms on top of the chicory and the rabbit pieces on top of the mushrooms. Garnish with delicate sprigs of chervil and serve at once.

Tian of tomatoes with vegetables à la Grecque

MOULDS OF MARINATED FRESH TOMATOES FILLED WITH AUBERGINE CAVIAR AND SERVED WITH TENDER BABY VEGETABLES LIGHTLY INFUSED WITH SAFFRON AND CORIANDER BALSAMIC DRESSING. EXCELLENT AS A FIRST COURSE IN SUMMER.

1 Have ready the Aubergine Caviar and set aside.
2 Skin the tomatoes by dipping briefly in boiling water so that the skins slip off easily. Cut each into quarters and discard the seeds.
3 Season and marinate in 3 tablespoons of the oil together with 1 teaspoon of the balsamic vinegar and half the herbs, for about 2 hours.
4 Prepare all the vegetables by peeling or trimming. Bring the remainder of the oil and vinegar to the boil, then add all the baby vegetables, the remaining herbs, and the crushed coriander seeds and saffron strands. Remove from the heat and leave to infuse, turning once or twice, until cool. Chill for at least 30 minutes before serving.
5 Drain the tomatoes, reserving the marinade. Use the tomatoes to line the base and sides of two ramekins. Spoon in the Aubergine Caviar, pressing it down firmly, then chill for about 30 minutes to allow it to settle.
6 To serve, unmould a tian into the centre of each plate and spoon over the reserved tomato marinade to glaze. Prepare the Mixed Salad Leaves and place small mounds on top. Drain the baby vegetables from their marinade, arrange them around each tian then trickle over a little of the marinade to garnish.

INGREDIENTS (for 2)

½ x quantity Aubergine Caviar (page 101)
6 large dark red plum tomatoes
200ml/7fl oz/⅞ cup olive oil
2 teaspoons balsamic vinegar
1 teaspoon each of chopped basil, chervil, coriander and chives
2 small servings Mixed Salad Leaves (page 54)
sea salt and freshly ground black pepper

FOR THE VEGETABLE GARNISH:

4 baby fennel bulbs, or 1 medium one cut into quarters
4 baby onions
4 baby carrots
4 baby leeks, or 1 medium one slit lengthways into four
4 baby turnips
4 asparagus tips
6 coriander seeds, crushed
1 good pinch saffron strands

Salad of spring vegetables with lemon vinaigrette

A VERY SIMPLE, LIGHT SALAD STARTER CONTAINING A HOST OF YOUNG, TENDER VEGETABLES, BLANCHED AND TOSSED IN A LIVELY LEMON AND SPICE VINAIGRETTE. THE SECRET OF THIS REFRESHING SALAD IS TO ALLOW THE BLANCHED COOKED VEGETABLES TO COOL IN THE DRESSING. IF SOME OF THE BABY VEGETABLES ARE DIFFICULT TO GET HOLD OF, BUY THE YOUNGEST YOU CAN FIND AND PEEL OFF A FEW LAYERS, OR CUT THEM INTO BITE-SIZED CHUNKS.

INGREDIENTS (for 2)

½ x quantity Basic Salad Vinaigrette (page 19)
juice of 1 lemon
12 coriander seeds, crushed
2 star anise
1 teaspoon each of chopped basil, chervil and chives
100g/3½oz baby carrots
100g/3½oz baby leeks
100g/3½oz baby turnips
100g/3½oz young asparagus
100g/3½oz baby fennel bulbs
150g/5oz Mixed Salad Leaves (page 54)
sea salt and freshly ground black pepper

1 Prepare the Basic Salad Vinaigrette and mix in the lemon juice, spices and half the herbs. Set aside.

2 Prepare all the vegetables apart from the Mixed Salad Leaves, leaving them whole and lightly peeling or scrubbing as necessary. Bring a large pan of salted water to the boil. Blanch all the vegetables together for just 1 minute, timing from when the water returns to the boil. You may find this easier to do in a blanching basket.

3 Drain and immediately toss in the Basic Salad Vinaigrette. Season lightly, if liked. Leave to cool completely, stirring the vegetables gently from time to time so that they absorb the flavourings evenly.

4 When cool, remove the vegetables from the dressing using a slotted spoon. Reserve the dressing.

5 Prepare the Mixed Salad Leaves and lightly dress with a little of the reserved Vinaigrette. Arrange the vegetables prettily around the salad. Lightly *nappe* (coat) with any remaining dressing so that everything glistens, and sprinkle over the remaining herbs.

Fillets of sardine and red mullet

IN THE SUMMER, WE SERVE THIS LIGHT DISH OF RED MULLET AND SARDINES WITH A COURT-BOUILLON OR VEGETABLE NAGE SAUCE AND TOMATO CONCASSE. FOR A MAIN COURSE, WE SERVE THIS WITH A WARM TOMATO AND BASIL TART (PAGE 75), AN IDEA I FIRST CAME ACROSS IN PARIS. IDEALLY, USE SMALL RED MULLETS FOR THIS DISH, SO THEY MATCH THE SARDINES IN SIZE. YOU WILL NEED TO ALLOW ONE SUCH MULLET PER PERSON. ALTERNATIVELY, BUY TWO LARGER MULLETS AND CUT EACH INTO 4 FILLETS. YOUR FISHMONGER SHOULD BE ABLE TO SCALE AND FILLET THEM FOR YOU.

INGREDIENTS (for 4)

200ml/7fl oz/⅞ cup Vegetable Nage (page 13) or Court-bouillon (page 16)

4 tablespoons Tomato Concasse (page 97)

4 small red mullets, scaled, gutted and filleted, or 2 large ones each cut into 4 fillets

4 fresh sardines, gutted and filleted

8 basil leaves

2-3 teaspoons olive oil

sea salt and freshly ground black pepper

1 Have ready the Vegetable Nage or Court-bouillon and the Tomato Concasse; set aside.

2 Trim the fish fillets to neaten with a small sharp knife then pull out any pin bones using tweezers. Place in a shallow pan or deep frying pan and season well.

3 Pour over the Vegetable Nage or Court-bouillon, bring up to the boil then leave the mullets and sardines to cool down, while still in the liquid.

4 When cold, remove the fish carefully and chill. Strain the Vegetable Nage or Court-bouillon then add half the basil leaves and leave to infuse. Chop the remaining basil leaves into fine julienne.

5 Mix the Tomato Concasse into the flavoured Vegetable Nage or the Court-bouillon.

6 To serve, arrange the mullets and sardines in the centre of chilled plates. Strain the Vegetable Nage or Court-bouillon through a sieve, reserving the Tomato Concasse, and use to glaze the fish. Sprinkle the Tomato Concasse and julienne of basil all around. Finally, drizzle over the olive oil.

Fillets of sardine

and red mullet

Tomato and basil tarts

FULL OF FLAVOUR AND VERY VERSATILE, THESE LIGHT, CRISP, TARTS PILED HIGH WITH JUICY TOMATO SLICES AND DRIZZLED WITH BASIL-FLAVOURED OIL CAN BE SERVED AS A FIRST COURSE OR VEGETABLE ACCOMPANIMENT. THEY ARE ESPECIALLY GOOD SERVED WITH FILLETS OF SARDINE AND RED MULLET (PAGE 72).

INGREDIENTS (for 4)

200g/7oz homemade Puff Pastry (page 25)
500g/1lb 2oz plump ripe tomatoes
25g/1oz/½ cup basil leaves, cut into fine julienne strips
100ml/3½oz/½ cup olive oil
1 tablespoon balsamic vinegar
sea salt and freshly ground black pepper

1 On a lightly floured board, roll out the Puff Pastry to a thickness of about 3mm/⅛in. Cut out four 10cm/4in circles, prick them with a fork and leave to rest in the refrigerator for 20 minutes.

2 Preheat the oven to 220°C/425°F/Gas Mark 7. Place the pastry circles on a baking sheet and place another baking sheet on top. Bake for 5 minutes. Remove the top baking sheet, turn the discs over using a palette knife, replace the top sheet and bake for a further 5 minutes.

3 Remove the top sheet completely and bake the circles once again until a light golden colour. Remove and reduce the oven temperature to 190°C/375°F/Gas Mark 5.

4 Skin the tomatoes by dipping them briefly into boiling water then slipping off the skins. Using a sharp knife, cut into very thin slices. Arrange the tomatoes on each tart in a circle of overlapping slices, building each up into a high mound in the centre. Season well.

5 Sprinkle half of the basil over the tarts and drizzle over half the oil. Return to the oven and bake for a further 6–7 minutes, glazing every 2 minutes with a little more of the oil. Remove from the oven and drizzle the remaining oil over the tarts along with the balsamic vinegar and the last of the basil. Serve warm.

Tomato and basil tarts

Pasta and risotto

What I love most of all about fresh pasta and risotto is the reward you receive in relation to the effort you have invested. You can change your ravioli and tortellini fillings and risotto flavourings as you do your clothes, according to the seasons and to your mood. You will find the basic method for making Pasta Dough in the Building Blocks chapter (page 27).

Ravioli and tortellini are very personal. The secret is to use a very thin pasta dough with a moist, chunky filling that should be just cooked in the centre – no more. The technique may need a little practice as the edges must be sufficiently well sealed to prevent any water from penetrating the pasta coating during cooking and ruining the filling.

With risotto, you must use an authentic round-grained Italian risotto rice that cooks to a silky creaminess yet retains a firm al dente *bite. Carnaroli, Arborio or Vialone Nano grains are what we prefer. Risotto can be flavoured with mascarpone cheese, freshly grated Parmesan cheese and just a hint of Shallot Confit (page 94): nothing too strong or overpowering.*

Ravioli of lobster with its own vinaigrette

A VERY SPECIAL LIGHT MEAL AND AN IDEAL USE FOR LOBSTERS WITH DAMAGED CLAWS, SINCE THE RECIPE REQUIRES ONLY THE LOBSTER MEAT RATHER THAN A PERFECT PRESENTATION IN THE SHELL. THE LOBSTER MEAT, COMBINED WITH SALMON AND HERBS, FORMS THE FILLING FOR THE RAVIOLI. THESE RAVIOLI CAN BE ASSEMBLED AND BLANCHED IN ADVANCE, THEN SET ASIDE, TO BE FINISHED JUST BEFORE SERVING.

INGREDIENTS (for 4)

FOR THE RAVIOLI:

2 live baby lobsters, each weighing about 500g/1lb 2oz

100g/3½oz fresh salmon fillet

½ teaspoon each chopped fresh basil, tarragon and chervil

about ¼ x quantity (200g/7oz) homemade Pasta Dough (page 27)

sea salt and freshly ground black pepper

FOR THE VEGETABLE GARNISH:

1 small Savoy cabbage

50g/2oz/½ stick butter

100g/3½oz carrots

FOR THE VINAIGRETTE:

200 ml/7fl oz/⅞ cup Langoustine Stock or Lobster Stock (page 15)

5 tablespoons olive oil

½ teaspoon each chopped basil, tarragon and chervil

1 To kill the lobsters, lay them stomach downwards on a board, then pierce firmly through the cross marks on their skulls with the tip of a heavy, sharp knife. Remove the claws, slit the bodies in half lengthways and clean the insides, removing the entrails and coral. Blanch the body tails and claws in boiling water for 15 seconds; this helps release the meat from the shell. Drain, remove the meat from the bodies and claws, then dry with a tea towel or kitchen paper towel. Chop into fine dice and place in the refrigerator.

2 In a food processor, blend the salmon fillet to a smooth purée. Mix together the purée, the diced lobster meat, the herbs and some seasoning.

3 To complete the ravioli filling, divide the mixture into 8 neat, round balls, rolling them with hands that are completely dry. This may be a little sticky, but it is essential not to get any moisture in the filling. Place the balls on a plate and chill to firm.

4 For the ravioli, roll out the Pasta Dough thinly; then using a 10cm/4in cutter, stamp out 16 circles and fill them with the chilled balls to make 8 filled ravioli (steps 1-4, page 29). Blanch and refresh the ravioli (steps 9-10, page 28), Drain well, cover and chill until required.

5 Meanwhile, prepare the vegetable garnish: cut the cabbage into fine shreds and sauté in a pan with half the butter until just wilted. Peel the carrots then cut into fine julienne strips. Sauté these separately in the remaining butter until wilted and just softened, and keep warm.

6 For the vinaigrette, boil the Langoustine or Lobster Stock until reduced by about two-thirds. Add the oil and the herbs, then set aside to infuse.

7 Just prior to serving, reheat the ravioli in boiling water for 2 minutes then drain. Place a mound of the cabbage in the centre of each warmed plate. Top each with a ravioli and arrange the julienne of carrot on top of each ravioli. Spoon the vinaigrette over and around the ravioli then serve.

Ravioli of lobster

with its own vinaigrette

Ravioli of goat's cheese with artichoke bouillon

GOAT'S CHEESE, BLENDED WITH A SMALL AMOUNT OF MASCARPONE CHEESE, MAKES A TANGY, LIGHT FILLING FOR RAVIOLI – AN IDEAL GARNISH PARTNER FOR A CLEAR BROTH OR BOUILLON OF GLOBE ARTICHOKES, SOPHISTICATED YET SIMPLE. BOTH GARNISH AND BOUILLON CAN BE MADE IN ADVANCE AND REHEATED JUST PRIOR TO SERVING. FOLLOW THE INSTRUCTIONS FOR MAKING RAVIOLI ON PAGE 29, BUT INSTEAD OF SHAPING THE FILLING INTO BALLS, PIPE THE CREAMED GOAT'S CHEESE ONTO EACH PASTA DISC.

INGREDIENTS (for 6)

FOR THE RAVIOLI:

about ⅓ x quantity (300g/10½oz) homemade Pasta Dough (page 27)
200g/7oz soft goat's cheese e.g. crottin
2 tablespoons mascarpone cheese
1 egg yolk beaten with a pinch of salt and 2 teaspoons water

FOR THE BOUILLON:

1 litre/1¾ pints/4½ cups Chicken Stock (page 18) or Vegetable Nage (page 13)
4 large globe artichokes
juice of ½ lemon
3 tablespoons olive oil
6 shallots, sliced
12 black peppercorns
3 tablespoons dry white wine
1 teaspoon each of chopped tarragon, basil and chives
sea salt and freshly ground white pepper

1 Have ready the Pasta Dough and Chicken Stock or Vegetable Nage, and set both aside.

2 For the ravioli, roll out the Pasta Dough (steps 1-2, page 29) then stamp out 12 circles using a 10cm/4in cutter. For the ravioli filling, mash the goat's cheese with a wooden spoon to soften, then beat in the mascarpone cheese until smooth. Place in a piping bag fitted with a plain 1cm/½in nozzle and pipe the mixture onto 6 of the pasta discs. Finish making the ravioli according to the instructions on page 29, using the beaten egg wash to seal. Blanch (steps 9-10, page 28) and plunge into iced water. Set aside.

3 For the bouillon, prepare the artichokes in the same way as for the Velouté of Artichokes with Foie Gras (step 2, page 47).

4 Heat the oil in a saucepan and sauté the shallots and drained artichoke slices along with the peppercorns until the vegetables are nicely browned and caramelized, about 10 minutes.

5 Deglaze the pan with the wine then add the stock. Bring to the boil then simmer for about 15 minutes. Remove from the heat and leave the vegetables to infuse for 30 minutes.

6 Line a colander with damp muslin or a clean tea towel. Pour the bouillon through twice, or until you have a clear broth. Set aside until you are ready to serve.

7 To serve, return the bouillon to the boil, stir in the chopped herbs and check the seasoning. Add the reserved ravioli and simmer very gently to reheat. Serve immediately.

Tagliatelle with truffles

SIMPLE AND SUBLIME – WHEN FRESH TRUFFLES ARE IN SEASON THERE IS LITTLE TO BEAT THEIR EXQUISITE FLAVOUR AND THEIR GLORIOUS PARTNERSHIP WITH FRESH PASTA. IN THE RESTAURANT, WE LIKE TO USE TRUFFLES SHAVED INTO THE THINNEST SLICES, THEN SCATTERED ON TOP OF A DISH, IN THIS CASE HOMEMADE TAGLIATELLE ACCOMPANIED BY A WILD MUSHROOM SAUCE. YOU NEED ONLY ONE SMALL TRUFFLE OF ABOUT 20-30G/¾-1OZ FOR THIS DISH. IT WOULD MAKE A DIVINE STARTER.

BUYING FRESH TRUFFLES

THE TRUFFLE SEASON STARTS IN LATE OCTOBER AND LASTS UNTIL MARCH. TRUFFLES ARE VERY EXPENSIVE AROUND CHRISTMAS, WHEN DEMAND IS HIGH IN FRANCE, AND PRICES WILL REFLECT THIS. THE BEST TIME FOR BUYING IS IN JANUARY AND FEBRUARY. IN THE RESTAURANT WE USE THE BLACK TRUFFLE FROM THE PÉRIGORD REGION IN SOUTH-WEST FRANCE FOR SAUCES AND SOUPS, ADDING SMALL SHAVINGS AS A GARNISH, AS ON OUR CAPPUCCINO SOUPS (PAGES 32-35); AND WE USE THE WHITE TRUFFLE FROM ALBA IN ITALY FOR PASTA, SALADS AND FOR VARIOUS FORMS OF GARNISH. SPECIALLY DESIGNED TRUFFLE SHAVERS ARE IDEAL FOR PRODUCING TRANSPARENT, WAFER-THIN SLICES. IN PLACE OF ONE OF THESE, YOU MIGHT TRY A MANDOLIN SLICER OR A VERY SHARP KNIFE BUT, QUITE HONESTLY, HAVING INVESTED IN A TRUFFLE, YOU MAY FIND IT WORTHWHILE INVESTING IN A PROPER TRUFFLE SHAVER.

WHETHER BLACK OR WHITE, A PERFECT TRUFFLE SHOULD BE HIGHLY PERFUMED AND, GENERALLY, THE SMALLER IT IS, THE MORE INTENSE ITS GLORIOUS SCENT. CHECK THE TRUFFLE FOR WORMS – IT SHOULD BE BLEMISH-FREE AND UNCORRODED. FINALLY, BE WARNED – A GOOD TRUFFLE IS EXPENSIVE, BUT A LITTLE GOES A LONG WAY. ONCE PURCHASED, STORE YOUR TRUFFLE FOR UP TO ABOUT 3 WEEKS IN A BAG OF RISOTTO RICE IN THE REFRIGERATOR. NOT ONLY DOES IT KEEP THE TRUFFLE AT ITS BEST, IT ALSO IMPARTS A HEAVENLY SCENT TO THE RICE!

INGREDIENTS (for 4)

250g/9oz homemade Tagliatelle (page 29) or fresh ready-made
150ml/¼ pint/¾ cup Vegetable Nage (page 13) or vegetable cooking water
100ml/3½fl oz/½ cup double cream
100g/3½oz wild mushrooms, sliced
2 tablespoons truffle oil
20-30g/¾-1oz fresh truffle
sea salt and freshly ground black pepper

1 Cook homemade Tagliatelle briefly in boiling lightly salted water for no more than 1 minute. Cook ready-made tagliatelle according to the pack instructions. Drain, then toss in the Vegetable Nage or vegetable water, and the cream. Season and keep warm in the pan.

2 Gently fry the sliced mushrooms in the truffle oil until just tender, about 2-3 minutes, stirring well.

3 Arrange the pasta on warmed plates, add the mushrooms and grate or finely shave over the truffle. Serve immediately.

Tortellini of ratatouille

Tortellini of ratatouille with sauce gazpacho

This dish has all the punchy flavour you would expect from its Mediterranean ingredients – peppers, courgettes, aubergines, olives and olive oil. The Pasta Dough, ratatouille and sauce gazpacho can all be made in advance, then brought together for serving, finished with a flourish of deep-fried celeriac shreds.

INGREDIENTS (for 4)

½ head celeriac
vegetable oil for frying
Mixed Salad Leaves (page 54)
1 tablespoon Tapenade (page 19)
1 tablespoon olive oil
sea salt and freshly ground black pepper

FOR THE TORTELLINI:

½ x quantity (425g/15oz) homemade Pasta Dough (page 27)
2 tablespoons Tomato Concasse (page 97)
85g/3oz red pepper, very finely diced
85g/3oz courgette, very finely diced
85g/3oz aubergine, very finely diced
2 tablespoons olive oil
1 large basil leaf, sliced into fine julienne strips
200g/7oz young spinach leaves
50g/2oz/½ cup pitted black olives, puréed

FOR THE SAUCE GAZPACHO:

500g/1lb 2oz/4 cups ripe cherry tomatoes
2 tablespoon double cream
50g/2oz/½ stick butter, diced
2 tablespoons olive oil

1 Have ready the Pasta Dough and the Tomato Concasse, and set aside.

2 To make the tortelloni filling, sauté the diced peppers, courgette and aubergine in the oil for about 5 minutes until just cooked. Drain and squeeze dry, either in a large piece of muslin or a clean tea towel.

3 Leave the mixture to cool, then place in a bowl and mix in the Tomato Concasse and the sliced basil. Season, then shape into 24 small balls and chill to firm up.

4 Blanch the spinach until just wilted, then drain and pat dry gently on a clean cloth, keeping the leaves whole if possible. Spoon the puréed olives over each ratatouille ball, and wrap each lightly in a spinach leaf. Set aside.

5 To assemble the tortellini, roll out the Pasta Dough. Using a 9cm/3½in cutter, cut out 24 circles, then fill each with a spinach-wrapped ball, folding and curling into a tortellini shape (steps 1-8, page 28). Blanch and set aside until required (steps 9-10, page 28).

6 To make the sauce gazpacho, blend the cherry tomatoes to a purée in a food processor or liquidizer, then rub through a sieve set over a saucepan. Boil gently to reduce by half. Add the cream plus the diced butter and the oil. Purée again and rub through the sieve a second time. Season to taste and set aside.

7 Peel the celeriac and cut into fine julienne strips. Heat about 2cm/¾in of vegetable oil in a deep sauté pan, then fry the celeriac until golden-brown and crisp. Drain well.

8 To serve, prepare the Mixed Salad Leaves and arrange in the centre of the serving dishes. Blanch the tortellini again for about 2 minutes then drain and arrange around the salad. Mix the Tapenade with the tablespoon of oil. Finish the sauce gazpacho by warming it through then spoon it around the tortellini, followed by the Tapenade mixture. Arrange the celeriac on top of each tortellini and serve straight away.

with sauce gazpacho

Cannelloni of crab in a shellfish soup

SOME PEOPLE MAY FIND CANNELLONI A TOUCH HARDER TO MAKE THAN RAVIOLI BUT I THINK IT IS WORTH PERSEVERING. THE FILLING HERE IS MADE FROM FRESH, SHREDDED CRAB, HELD TOGETHER WITH A PURÉE OF RAW SALMON. THE FINISHED CANNELLONI ARE THEN SERVED IN A SOUP OF SCALLOPS AND OYSTERS. SERVE AS A STARTER OR A MAIN COURSE.

1 Have ready the Pasta Dough and Fish Velouté and set aside. For the cannelloni filling, blend the salmon to a fine purée in a food processor. If it is easier, use more salmon than required, then weigh out the required 25g/1oz. The remainder can be frozen.

2 Using a wooden spoon, cream the salmon purée in a bowl to soften. Check the crab meat for any minute pieces of shell then beat it into the salmon along with the basil, cream and seasoning. Spoon into a piping bag with a plain 1.5cm/⅝in nozzle and set in the refrigerator to chill.

3 Roll out the pasta as for ravioli (page 29), then cut out four 10 x 15cm/4 x 6in strips. It is worth cutting out a few extra to allow for mistakes or excess filling.

4 Bring a large pan of salted water to the boil, blanch the pasta sheets for 10 seconds then immediately plunge into a bowl of ice-cold water. Drain and pat dry on a clean, dry tea towel.

5 Tear off a sheet of cling film for each pasta sheet, place the pasta on it then pipe the filling, widthways, just above the centre. Roll up like a cigar making sure it is nice and tight. Twist then knot the ends of the cling film to seal; this will hold the filling in place. Place in the refrigerator to firm. Repeat with the remaining sheets and filling.

6 When set, blanch the cannelloni, still wrapped in cling film, in gently boiling water for 4 minutes, then drain.

7 For the soup, bring the Fish Velouté up to the boil. Add the oysters and poach them gently for about 30 seconds; add the scallops and oyster juices. Heat for another 30 seconds then check the seasoning and stir in the chervil.

8 To serve, unwrap the cannelloni and discard the cling film. Place one in the centre of each warmed soup bowl, spoon over the oysters and scallops and pour over the soup. Serve immediately.

INGREDIENTS (for 2-4)

FOR THE CANNELLONI:

about ¼ x quantity (200g/7oz) homemade Pasta Dough (page 27)

25g/1oz fresh, raw salmon, beaten to a purée

100g/3½oz fresh cooked white crab meat

1 teaspoon chopped basil

50ml/2fl oz/¼ cup double cream

FOR THE SOUP:

500ml/18fl oz/2 cups Fish Velouté (page 14)

4 oysters, removed from their shells, juices reserved (page 36)

4 medium scallops, shelled, trimmed and washed (page 40), chopped into fine dice

2 teaspoons chopped chervil

sea salt and freshly ground black pepper

Risotto of tomato confit and roasted cèpes

SIMPLE, BUT PERFECT. RISOTTO IS A DELICIOUSLY COMFORTING DISH AND, CONTRARY TO POPULAR OPINION, IT CAN BE MADE PARTLY IN ADVANCE THEN FINISHED JUST AS YOU ARE ABOUT TO SERVE. I PREFER TO USE THE CARNAROLI GRAIN OF RISOTTO RICE, BUT AN ARBORIO OR VIALONE NANO WILL DO. RICE SIMPLY LABELLED 'RISOTTO', WITHOUT A VARIETY NAME, WILL NOT HAVE THE SAME *AL DENTE* BITE. THE METHOD BELOW IS FOR COOKING RISOTTO IN ADVANCE OF SERVING BUT YOU CAN, OF COURSE, SERVE IT FRESHLY COOKED FOR A QUICK, SIMPLE MEAL.

INGREDIENTS (for 3-4 as a main course)

FOR THE RISOTTO:

500ml/18fl oz/2 cups Chicken Stock (page 18) or Vegetable Nage (page 13)
2 large shallots, finely chopped
3 tablespoons olive oil
200g/7oz/1 cup risotto rice e.g. Carnaroli, Arborio or Vialone Nano
100ml/3½fl oz/½ cup dry white wine
2 tablespoons mascarpone cheese
25g/1oz/½ cup freshly grated Parmesan cheese

FOR THE FLAVOURINGS:

250g/9oz Tomato Confit (page 98)
200g/7oz fresh cèpes or chestnut variety of mushrooms (champignons de Paris)
4 tablespoons olive oil
1 tablespoon each of finely chopped basil, chives and chervil
sea salt and freshly ground black pepper

1 Put the Chicken Stock or Vegetable Nage in a saucepan and bring to the boil. Set aside.

2 In a medium saucepan, gently sauté the shallots in 3 tablespoons of oil for about 2 minutes or until softened. Stir in the rice and cook for a further 2 minutes to seal the rice.

3 Stir in the wine and deglaze the pan. Cook until the liquid has reduced to a syrupy consistency.

4 Meanwhile, reheat the Chicken Stock or Vegetable Nage and bring to a gentle simmer. Add to the rice one ladleful at a time, stirring well and adding more stock only when each addition has been absorbed. Cook until just a touch soft, usually about 10 minutes.

5 Strain the rice through a sieve set over a bowl, reserving the liquid for later use. Spread the rice out on a tray. When it is cool, cover and set it aside until ready to reheat and serve.

6 Meanwhile, slice the cèpes or mushrooms and heat 4 tablespoons of olive oil in a frying pan. Sauté the cèpes on both sides until golden brown, about 5 minutes. Remove with a slotted spoon and set aside some of the neatly shaped ones for use as a garnish. Reserve the pan juices.

7 When ready to serve, have ready the Tomato Confit. Return the rice to the saucepan with 2 tablespoons of its reserved cooking liquid, stirring well. Cook for about 3 minutes, adding extra liquid if the rice looks a little thick. Quickly mix in the mascarpone and the Parmesan, stirring until light and creamy. Check the seasoning.

8 Fold in the Tomato Confit, the cèpes (except those reserved for the garnish) and the herbs.

9 Transfer the risotto to warmed bowls, garnish with the remaining cèpes, drizzle over the pan juices of the cèpes and serve straight away.

Risotto of baby clams

SOMETIMES SPECIALITY FISHMONGERS HAVE SMALL, LIGHT BROWN BABY CLAMS FOR SALE. IF YOU SPOT THEM, THIS IS AN IDEAL RECIPE FOR EXPLOITING THEIR SPECIAL QUALITIES.

INGREDIENTS (for 3-4 as a main course)

FOR THE RISOTTO:

500ml/18fl oz/2 cups Fish Stock (page 14) plus a little extra for reheating
2 large shallots, finely chopped
3 tablespoons olive oil plus extra for serving
200g/7oz/1 cup risotto rice e.g. Carnaroli, Arborio or Vialone Nano variety
50ml/2fl oz/¼ cup dry white wine
1 tablespoon mascarpone cheese
1 tablespoon freshly grated Parmesan cheese

FOR THE FLAVOURINGS:

200g/7oz fresh baby clams
50ml/2fl oz/¼ cup dry white wine
1 bay leaf
2 tablespoons skinned and finely diced red pepper
2 tablespoons skinned and finely diced yellow pepper
50ml/2fl oz/¼ cup double cream, lightly whipped
1 teaspoon each of chopped chives and basil
few sprigs chervil
sea salt and freshly ground black pepper

1 Have ready the Fish Stock and set aside.

2 Check the clams and discard any that are opened. Wash the clams in plenty of cold water, scrubbing the shells with a small brush and changing the water two or three times. Drain. Place the clams in a saucepan with the wine and the bay leaf.

3 Cover with a tight-fitting lid and cook the clams for 2-3 minutes to steam them open, shaking the pan once or twice. Remove from the heat and discard any clams that have not opened. Drain through a colander set over a bowl, reserving the juices.

4 When the clams are cool enough to handle, remove the meat from the shells and set aside.

5 Blanch the diced peppers briefly in boiling water until just softened, plunge into ice-cold water and drain.

6 Make the risotto base in the same way as for the Risotto of Tomato Confit and Roasted Cèpes (steps 1-5, page 85) substituting Fish Stock for the Chicken Stock or Vegetable Nage.

7 Complete the risotto (step 7, page 85) incorporating the reserved clam juices before adding the mascarpone and the Parmesan. Mix in the diced peppers and the whipped cream. Reheat gently and check the seasoning.

8 Reheat the clams in a little stock and add the chives and basil. Arrange the risotto in the centre of warmed plates and spoon around the clams. Drizzle over a little olive oil and garnish with chervil sprigs. Serve straight away.

Risotto of baby clams

Risotto of herbs with roasted baby scallops

THIS IS MADE USING THE BASIC RISOTTO METHOD AS FOR THE RISOTTO OF TOMATO CONFIT AND ROASTED CÈPES (PAGE 85) USING FISH STOCK INSTEAD OF CHICKEN STOCK OR VEGETABLE NAGE, AND USING WHOLE OR SLICED PAN-FRIED SCALLOPS INSTEAD OF CÈPES. THE SCALLOPS CAN BE INCLUDED IN THIS DISH IN ONE OF THREE WAYS: EITHER WHOLE, IF BABY SCALLOPS, SLICED IN HALF, SAUTÉED QUICKLY IN OLIVE OIL AND SERVED ON TOP OF THE RISOTTO, OR DICED AND SAUTÉED IN OLIVE OIL THEN STIRRED IN AT THE END.

INGREDIENTS (for 3-4 as a main course)

FOR THE RISOTTO:

500ml/18fl oz/2 cups Fish Stock (page 14)
2 large shallots, finely chopped
3 tablespoons olive oil plus extra for sautéeing and serving
200g/7oz/1 cup risotto rice e.g. Carnaroli, Arborio or Vialone Nano variety
50ml/2fl oz/¼ cup dry white wine
1 tablespoon mascarpone cheese
1 tablespoon freshly grated Parmesan cheese

FOR THE FLAVOURINGS:

30 baby or 8-9 medium scallops, shelled, trimmed and washed (page 40)
50ml/2fl oz/¼ cup double cream, lightly whipped
1 teaspoon each of chopped tarragon, chives and basil
2 tablespoons balsamic vinegar
sea salt and freshly ground black pepper

1 Have ready the Fish Stock and set aside.

2 If you are using medium scallops either slice in half for use as a garnish or dice them so that they can be incorporated into the risotto. Set aside.

3 Make the risotto base in the same way as for the Risotto of Tomato Confit and Roasted Cèpes (steps 1-5, page 85) substituting Fish Stock for the Chicken Stock or Vegetable Nage.

4 Heat a pan with a little oil then sauté whole or sliced scallops for 1 minute each side, diced scallops for no more than 2 minutes, stirring frequently; set aside.

5 Complete the risotto (step 7, page 85), adding the mascarpone and the Parmesan. Mix in the whipped cream and the fresh herbs. Check the seasoning. If using diced scallops stir them in at this stage. If using whole or sliced scallops, use as a garnish. Serve the risotto on warmed plates. Drizzle round a little olive oil followed by the balsamic vinegar and serve straight away.

Risotto of herbs with roasted baby scallops

Vegetables

Although I am known for my keen interest in main-course fish and meat dishes, I have a healthy respect for vegetables; and if you combine two or three of my vegetable ideas, replacing chicken or fish stocks with Vegetable Nage, you can achieve a fantastic main-course vegetarian dish.

This respect means that ninety-five per cent of my vegetables are cooked to order at the last minute, thereby retaining their vibrancy of colour and freshness of flavour. I also insist that my chefs pay great attention to the preparation of vegetables. With salads, only the prime tips of leaves are used, while spinach and broccoli are trimmed of their woody stalks. Appropriate selection is also crucial: the variety of potatoes, for instance, can make or break a dish.

About one-third of each main-course dish involves vegetables which, I admit, I use as garnish. But this is not to be left on the side of a plate. Rather it is to be considered integral to the dish itself because it enhances and complements the rest of the ingredients. Take my Tomato Confit (page 98), Potato Rösti (page 94) or Braised Salsify (page 92). These are worthy accompaniments with, say, roasted fish or pan-fried meat but, also, memorable in their own right. A good vegetable serving can elevate a course into the ethereal.

Braised salsify

WONDERFUL WITH SEA BASS AND A VARIETY OF ROASTED FISH. YOU MAY HAVE TO ORDER SALSIFY FROM YOUR GREENGROCER OR MAYBE YOU ALREADY GROW IT IN YOUR GARDEN. A MUCH UNDERVALUED VEGETABLE.

INGREDIENTS (for 6-8)

200ml/7fl oz/⅞ cup Fish Stock (page 14)
500g/1lb 2oz salsify
700ml/1¼ pints/3 cups cold water
100ml/3½fl oz/½ cup milk
juice of 1 lemon
1 tablespoon rock salt
50g/2oz/½ stick butter
1 fresh Bouquet Garni (page 18)
sea salt and ground white pepper

1 Have ready the Fish Stock and set aside.
2 Wash the salsify well, then peel, top and tail. Place immediately into a saucepan with the water, milk, lemon juice and rock salt.
3 Bring to the boil, then remove from the heat and leave the salsify to cool down in the milky water.
4 Drain, then cut into 4cm/1½in bâtons or thick julienne strips. Preheat the oven to 180°C/350°F/Gas Mark 4.
5 Heat the butter in a large, ovenproof frying pan or shallow, cast-iron casserole. Add the salsify bâtons and fry gently until they start to colour a little and caramelize.
6 Pour in the Fish Stock to just cover the salsify. Stir, add the Bouquet Garni and cook, uncovered, in the oven for 12-14 minutes until the liquid has evaporated and the salsify has become nicely glazed. Check the seasoning and serve.

Braised chicory

WHAT LITTLE BITTERNESS THERE IS IN RAW CHICORY IS ELIMINATED BY THIS COOKING PROCESS, WHICH ENSURES A SWEETISH EDGE. THE BRAISING ALSO GIVES THE CHICORY HEADS AN ATTRACTIVE, SYRUPY GLAZE. SERVE WITH SALMON, LAMB OR RABBIT.

INGREDIENTS (for 4-6 as an accompaniment)

200ml/7fl oz/⅞ cup Chicken Stock (page 18) or Fish Stock (page 14), to deglaze
8 medium heads chicory
3 tablespoons fresh lemon juice
3 tablespoons caster sugar
25g/1oz/¼ stick butter
sea salt and freshly ground black pepper

1 Have ready the Chicken or Fish Stock and set aside.
2 Trim the chicory of any bruised outside leaves, then trim the ends and use a small, sharp knife to remove the bitter core at the base of each head.
3 Bring a pan of water to the boil and add the lemon juice, 1 tablespoon of the sugar and salt to taste. Blanch the chicory for 8-10 minutes and drain well.
4 Arrange the heads in a single layer on a platter, sprinkle with the remaining sugar, and season with salt and pepper. Leave to cool for about 10 minutes.

5 Using your hands, gently squeeze each head to remove its bitter liquid; then set each head aside, draining them on kitchen paper towels if necessary.

6 In a large frying pan set over a moderately high heat, melt the butter and, when hot but not smoking, add the heads and brown evenly for about 2-3 minutes on each side.

7 Deglaze with a little stock, shaking the pan gently to coat the heads. Serve hot.

Glazed baby onions

USE THESE AS AN ACCOMPANIMENT FOR ROAST CHICKEN, LAMB OR GRILLED MEATS. IF THEY ARE AVAILABLE, CHOOSE SILVERSKIN ONIONS AS THEY HAVE THE FINEST FLAVOUR.

INGREDIENTS (for 8)

400g/14oz baby onions, ideally silverskin

15g/½ oz butter

1 teaspoon olive oil

1 tablespoon rock salt

1 bay leaf

1 sprig thyme

a little caster sugar, to sprinkle

1 Peel the onions and trim the roots. The peeling can be made easier by blanching the onions first in boiling water for one minute. The skins should then slip off readily. Preheat the oven to 180°C/350°F/Gas Mark 4.

2 In a heavy-based, ovenproof frying pan, heat the butter and oil, add the onions and shake the pan well to coat them.

3 Sprinkle over the salt, add the bay leaf and thyme, then sauté the onions over a medium heat until they acquire a pale golden colour.

4 Sprinkle lightly with sugar, and cover with a butter paper or a sheet of buttered greaseproof paper. Transfer to the oven. Cook for about 20 minutes – lifting the paper and turning the onions every 5 minutes or so – until the onions are tender in the centre and beginning to caramelize. Remove the bay leaf and thyme then serve.

Shallot confit

THIS IS USED IN SO MANY RECIPES IN THIS BOOK THAT IT IS WORTH MAKING UP A BATCH TO STORE IN THE REFRIGERATOR. IT IS, AFTER ALL, AN 'ACE' FLAVOURING, ESPECIALLY WHEN STIRRED INTO VINAIGRETTE. THE CONFIT IS BEST WHEN COOKED OVER THE LOWEST HEAT POSSIBLE. IF YOUR DOMESTIC HOB DOES NOT PERMIT SUCH CONTROL, THEN PLACE THE PAN ON A METAL HEAT-DIFFUSER.

INGREDIENTS (makes about 250ml/9fl oz/1 cup)

8-10 large shallots, roots trimmed
150ml/¼ pint/¾ cup extra-virgin olive oil
rock salt
1 sprig thyme
1 bay leaf

1 Using a large, sharp, cook's knife, chop the shallots into very fine dice.
2 Place in a heavy-based saucepan with the oil, a light sprinkling of salt, the thyme and bay leaf.
3 Set the pan over medium heat until the oil becomes hot, then adjust the heat to its lowest possible setting and continue to cook the shallots until they are meltingly tender – about 2 hours. Set aside to cool. Store in a screw-top jar in the refrigerator, where the confit will keep for up to one week, or, if covered with a layer of olive oil, for up to a month.

Potato rösti

PERFECT AS A LIGHT CRISP ACCOMPANIMENT TO MEAT, FISH OR VEGETABLES. YOU CAN MAKE POTATO RÖSTI AN HOUR OR TWO AHEAD AND EITHER KEEP THEM WARM, UNCOVERED IN A VERY LOW OVEN, OR REHEAT AS REQUIRED. CHOOSE A WAXY POTATO, SUCH AS MARIS PIPER OR PICASSO, THAT WILL HOLD ITS SHAPE DURING FRYING. WE COOK THESE FOUR AT A TIME USING 10CM/4IN DIAMETER METAL CUTTERS PLACED IN A LARGE FRYING PAN. HOWEVER, IF YOU DON'T HAVE ENOUGH CUTTERS OF THE SAME SIZE, SIMPLY MAKE THEM ONE AT A TIME. THEY TAKE JUST MINUTES TO COOK.

INGREDIENTS (for 4)

85g/3oz/¾ stick butter
500g/1lb 2oz waxy potatoes, peeled
sea salt

1 Clarify two-thirds of the butter. To do this, melt the butter slowly in a small pan, leave to stand off the heat for 2 minutes then carefully pour off the clear fat into a bowl, leaving behind the milky deposits, which can be thrown away. Cool.
2 Using a mandolin or the julienne cutter disc on your food processor, grate the potatoes into long thin julienne strips. Dry the strips by putting them into a clean cloth and squeezing hard. Transfer to a large bowl.

3 Season with salt to taste, then mix in the clarified butter. Leave to cool slightly to make the mixture easier to handle.

4 Heat a heavy-based frying pan until hot, then stand one or more plain metal cutters inside it. Press a quarter of the potato mixture down inside each cutter to make a neat round shape. As each Potato Rösti cooks, slide a little knob of the remaining butter down the side.

5 When the underside is golden brown, about 2 minutes, remove the metal cutter and flip over the Rösti with a palette knife. Cook the other side for a further 2-3 minutes or until crisp. Repeat with the remaining mixture and butter. Transfer the Rösti to kitchen paper towels and keep in a warm place until required.

Potato purée

THIS LIFTS MASHED POTATOES TO NEW HEIGHTS! THE SECRET LIES IN CHOOSING A FLOURY VARIETY OF POTATO SUCH AS DESIRÉE OR ROMANO, CUTTING THE POTATOES INTO EVEN-SIZED CHUNKS FOR EVEN COOKING, AND, FINALLY, IN USING A MOULI FOOD-MILL OR A POTATO-RICER FOR THE PURÉEING.

INGREDIENTS (makes about 1kg/2¼lb/4 cups)

4 large potatoes, weighing about 1kg/2¼lb, peeled and cut into 5cm/2in chunks

150ml/¼ pint/¾ cup double cream

85g/3oz/¾ stick unsalted butter, diced

freshly grated nutmeg

sea salt and ground white pepper

1 Rinse the chunks of potato well beneath cold running water to remove excess starch. Place them in a large saucepan, cover with cold water, add a tablespoon of salt and bring to the boil. Simmer gently until tender – usually 12-15 minutes. Drain the chunks well, return the potatoes to the pan, then set over gentle heat and shake the pan until any excess water has evaporated.

2 Ideally, purée the potatoes through a mouli food-mill or a potato-ricer. Alternatively, use a heavy masher but do not use a food processor, or the potatoes will turn gluey.

3 In a separate saucepan, boil the cream to reduce by half. Off the heat, beat the cream into the potato purée, then beat in the butter, nutmeg and seasoning to taste.

Tomato concasse

SKINNED, SEEDED AND FINELY DICED TOMATOES MAKE AN INVALUABLE ADDITION TO MANY OF MY RECIPES. TOMATO CONCASSE IS ALMOST INVARIABLY ADDED TOWARDS THE END OF MAKING A DISH, EITHER STIRRED INTO A SAUCE OR USED AS A GARNISH. USE RIPE, FULL-FLAVOURED PLUM TOMATOES WHERE POSSIBLE.

INGREDIENTS (makes about 300g/10½oz: 2 tomatoes will make about 100g/3½oz/ 4 tablespoons)

500g/1lb 2oz ripe plum tomatoes

1 Using a small, sharp knife, cut the core from the stalk end of each tomato, then slash the top of the opposite end to pierce the skin. Place the tomatoes in a bowl and cover with boiling water. Wait a minute or two until the skins start to curl, then drain off the water, run the tomatoes under cold water and skin.

2 Cut the tomatoes in half, remove the seeds and inner flesh then chop the flesh into very fine dice. Place in a bowl, cover and set aside in the fridge until required.

Tomato purée

QUITE DIFFERENT FROM CANNED TOMATO PURÉE! THIS IS MUCH LIGHTER IN TEXTURE AND COLOUR, WITH A LOVELY FRESH FLAVOUR. IT IS PARTICULARLY GOOD MIXED INTO AUBERGINE CAVIAR (PAGE 101). IF YOU HAVE ANY BASIL OR PARSLEY STALKS, ADD THEM DURING COOKING SO THEY IMPART ADDITIONAL FLAVOUR.

INGREDIENTS (makes about 600ml/1 pint)

1kg/2¼lb ripe tomatoes, preferably plum, skinned
100ml/3½fl oz/½ cup extra-virgin olive oil
3 shallots, sliced
2 cloves garlic, crushed
1 Bouquet Garni (page 18)

1 Preheat the oven to 180°C/350°F/Gas Mark 4. Quarter the tomatoes, then discard the seeds and core. Chop the flesh into large dice.

2 Heat the oil in a cast-iron or ovenproof saucepan and gently fry the shallots and garlic for 3-4 minutes until softened but not coloured.

3 Add the tomatoes, Bouquet Garni and herb stalks if using. Cover and transfer to the oven for about 50-60 minutes or until softened. Remove the Bouquet Garni and any herb stalks. Blend the tomato mixture to a smooth purée in a food processor. Cool and use as required.

STORAGE

THE PURÉE WILL KEEP FOR UP TO 3 DAYS IN A SCREW-TOP JAR IN THE REFRIGERATOR, LONGER IF COVERED WITH A LAYER OF OLIVE OIL. IT MAY ALSO BE FROZEN – IN BATCHES OF ABOUT 100ML/3½FL OZ/½ CUP – FOR UP TO 2 MONTHS.

Tomato concasse

Tomato confit

Discs of tomato flesh are slowly macerated in a low oven with fragrant olive oil, garlic and aromatic thyme for a delicious garnish or accompaniment.

INGREDIENTS (makes 75g/2½oz/¾ cup)

6 large plum tomatoes
olive oil, to drizzle over
2 cloves garlic, peeled and cut in slivers
1 large sprig thyme
freshly ground black pepper

1 Using a small, sharp knife, cut the core from the stalk end of each tomato, then slash the top of the opposite end to pierce the skin. Place the tomatoes in a bowl and cover with boiling water. Wait a minute or two until the skins start to curl, then drain off the water, run the tomatoes under cold water and skin.

2 Preheat the oven to the lowest possible setting, around 80°C/170°F/Gas Mark Low. Halve and seed the skinned tomatoes then cut out the inner ribs.

3 Using a round or oval pastry cutter, about 4cm/1½in in diameter, cut out one shape per tomato half. Lay flat, skinned side up, on a small shallow tray and trickle with olive oil.

4 Scatter over the garlic slivers. Pick the leaf tips off the sprig of thyme and sprinkle over the tomatoes then place in the oven.

5 Leave for 1-2 hours, brushing once or twice with the olive oil, until the tomatoes have softened but still hold their shape. Season with ground black pepper, cool, then transfer to a dish. Cover and chill until required.

Tomato confit

Little stuffed cabbage leaves

WE SERVE THESE AS A GARNISH FOR PIGEON BUT THEY ARE ALSO GOOD WITH A RANGE OF POULTRY, GAME AND MEAT DISHES. EACH BALL OF CABBAGE LEAF ENCLOSES A LITTLE OF OUR MIXTURE FOR THE TERRINE OF FOIE GRAS WITH CANARD CONFIT (PAGE 63). AT HOME, YOU COULD USE YOUR OWN CREAMY PÂTÉ MIXTURE AND, INDEED, VEGETARIANS MIGHT LIKE TO SUBSTITUTE A FINELY CHOPPED MUSHROOM AND HERB MIXTURE.

INGREDIENTS (makes about 24 little balls, enough for 6-8)

12 large cabbage leaves, preferably Savoy
150g/5oz Terrine of Foie Gras with Canard Confit (page 63) or smooth liver pâté
2 teaspoons cream
1 teaspoon chopped chervil
sea salt and freshly ground black pepper

1 Blanch the cabbage leaves in boiling salted water for about 15 seconds until just wilted, then plunge into ice-cold water to refresh them and keep the colour.

2 Pat dry in a clean cloth. Using a plain 7.5cm/3in cutter, cut out about 24 circles from the leaves, avoiding the hard stalks.

3 Soften the mixture of the Terrine of Foie Gras with Canard Confit or liver pâté and beat in the cream, chervil and seasoning, if liked. Spoon into a piping bag with a small, plain nozzle.

4 Cut off a piece of cling film large enough to completely wrap one cabbage leaf, about 20cm/8in long. Arrange a cabbage leaf in the centre of the cling film, then put this in the palm of your hand. Pipe about 1 small teaspoon of foie gras or pâté into the centre of the leaf. Draw up the edges of the cling film with the leaf to make a ball shape, wrapping tightly so there are no air-pockets, and twisting the excess cling film into a top-knot. Repeat until all the leaves are filled and wrapped.

5 Blanch the leaves in boiling water for 3 minutes. Drain and, when cool enough to handle, cut off the cling film and serve.

Creamed parsley

SERVE AS A GARNISH FOR PAN-FRIED BEEF FILLETS, OR TRY IT WHISKED INTO FISH VELOUTÉ (PAGE 14) AS A VIBRANT PARTNER FOR COD.

INGREDIENTS (for 4)

2 large bunches curly-leaf parsley, weighing about 100g/3½oz
100g/3½oz large spinach leaves
50ml/2fl oz/¼ cup double cream
sea salt and ground white pepper

1 Pick off the stalks from the parsley and spinach, then wash the leaves thoroughly and drain.

2 Bring a pan of water to the boil and blanch the parsley and spinach for about 4 minutes, adding the parsley first, then the spinach 1 minute later.

3 Drain well, but do not refresh in cold water. To dry the leaves thoroughly, place them in a clean tea towel and wrap up tightly, squeezing out all the water.

4 In a small saucepan, boil down the cream until reduced by half.

5 Meanwhile, put the parsley and spinach into a food processor and blend to a purée. Add the reduced cream and seasoning to taste. Cool and use as required.

Aubergine caviar

ALMOST THE IDEAL ALL-ROUND VEGETABLE ACCOMPANIMENT, THIS SOFTENED AUBERGINE FLESH HAS SO MANY USES: SPOONED INTO BABY AUBERGINE SHELLS, IT MAKES AN EXCELLENT PARTNER FOR ROAST LAMB AND FOR ROASTED FISH SUCH AS FIRM-FLESHED MONKFISH. IT IS ALSO A VERSATILE BASE FOR A RANGE OF VEGETARIAN MAIN COURSES, AND, MIXED WITH A LITTLE GRATED, FRESH HORSERADISH, IT EVEN MAKES A GOOD STARTER.

INGREDIENTS (makes about 450ml/¾ pint/1¾ cups)

1 medium aubergine
rock salt
1 large clove garlic, partially crushed
1 sprig rosemary

1 Preheat the oven to 220°C/425°F/Gas Mark 7. Halve the aubergine lengthways, score the flesh and sprinkle both cut sides with salt.

2 Lay the garlic and rosemary on one half, sandwich with the other, then wrap well in foil.

3 Bake for about 45 minutes, then lower the heat to 110°C/230°F/Gas Mark ¼, and bake for a further 20 minutes until the skins have shrivelled, the shells have collapsed and the flesh is completely soft.

4 Unwrap, scrape out the garlic and rosemary and discard. Scoop out the aubergine flesh onto a board. When cool enough to handle, chop the flesh very finely with a large sharp knife and place the pulp in a shallow saucepan.

5 Over a medium heat, stir the pulp until its excess moisture has evaporated, leaving the pulp – or 'caviar' – perfectly dried out. Use as required.

Fish and seafood

I have always been fascinated by fish and seafood, and they are a major part of my menu, especially in the summer. Maybe it's the sheer diversity of their varieties that excites me, their creative potential derived from the vibrancy of their colours, variation of textures and range of flavours.

When I go out to eat, most of the time I choose fish, perhaps because, subconsciously, I prefer a fish caught the previous day to a three-week-old beef fillet. When I cook with fish, I like to keep the dish simple and tamper with it as little as possible, roasting the fish just with oil and lemon, or steaming over a well-flavoured Court-bouillon. I also spend a lot of time preparing fish, trimming, checking meticulously for pin bones, then wrapping in cling film and chilling before cooking – a process that enhances the shape and firms the flesh.

My favourite fish is sea bass – in fact, it's my signature dish – served with a light vanilla velouté sauce. But I also harbour a great love for shellfish and buy most of my supplies from Scotland, including Belon oysters with their big, dark shells, so fresh they are difficult to prise open. Scallops I buy from suppliers who herd rather than farm them and, again, so fresh that when opened they still pulsate.

I find four good uses for scallops: the skirt is used in a stock; the small side muscles are added to velouté sauces; the coral is dried and ground to a powder to flavour risottos; and, finally, the sweet main meat is usually lightly pan-fried, often split in two if very meaty.

Fillet of sea bass

Fillet of sea bass with jus vanille

THIS HAS BEEN A SPECIALITY FOR US EVER SINCE WE OPENED. SOME WOULD SAY IT HAS BECOME OUR SIGNATURE DISH, AND MANY REGULAR CLIENTS RING IN ADVANCE TO FIND OUT WHETHER IT IS ON THE MENU. I FIRST EXPERIENCED IT AS AN IDEA IN PARIS, WHERE IT WAS LOBSTER THAT WAS BEING SERVED IN PARTNERSHIP WITH A VANILLA SAUCE. I FELT THE FLAVOURS WOULD BE QUITE FANTASTIC ENHANCED WITH BRAISED SALSIFY, WHICH IS AT ITS BEST IN THE AUTUMN. WHEN SALSIFY IS OUT OF SEASON, I SOMETIMES SERVE THE SEA BASS ON A BED OF SPINACH OR, AS I PREFER WHEN IT IS AVAILABLE, SWISS CHARD – AN UNDERRATED VEGETABLE THAT REQUIRES MORE CHAMPIONING. ASK YOUR FISHMONGER TO FILLET THE BASS BUT NOT TO SKIN IT AS THE SKIN HAS A BEAUTIFUL SILVER-GREY SHEEN THAT I LIKE TO SHOW OFF IN THE PRESENTATION OF THE DISH.

INGREDIENTS (for 4)

1 litre/1¾ pints/4½ cups Fish Stock (page 14)
1 sea bass weighing just over 1kg/2lb 4oz, filleted but not skinned
1 large vanilla pod
400g/14oz salsify
juice of 1 lemon
50g/2oz/½ stick butter plus an extra knob of ice-cold butter for finishing the sauce
8 whole baby fennel bulbs or 1 large bulb, halved, cored and sliced
1 sprig thyme
1 bay leaf
about 2 tablespoons olive oil
1 tablespoon double cream
sea salt, freshly ground black pepper and My Special Pepper Mix (page 106)

1 Have ready the Fish Stock and set aside.

2 Cut the sea bass fillets into 4 'tranches', or neat slices, then very lightly score the skin with a sharp knife. This will help the skin to caramelize during cooking and also prevent it from curling. If preparing ahead, wrap tightly in cling film (right).

3 Strain the Fish Stock through a fine sieve into a saucepan and bring it to the boil. Split the vanilla pod open and scrape the seeds into the hot stock, followed by the pod. Leave the stock to cool completely and the vanilla to infuse, then boil down to reduce by one-third. Remove and discard the pod.

4 To prepare the salsify, peel it thinly, then immediately drop it into cold water with a little of the lemon juice added to prevent discoloration. Blanch in boiling salted water for 2 minutes, drain, refresh in ice-cold water and drain again. Pat dry and cut into neat bâtons.

5 Melt half the butter in a saucepan and add a ladleful of the vanilla-flavoured stock. Bring to a light boil, toss in the salsify bâtons and cook until the stock has reduced to a glossy glaze. Stir in one-third of the remaining butter. The bâtons should be lightly coloured; if they are not, cook for a further minute or so. Set aside.

▶

MAKING FISH TRANCHES:

TRIMMING AND YET MORE TRIMMING – THIS IS THE SECRET OF GOOD PRESENTATION, ESPECIALLY FOR FISH. TRIM THE SIDES OF FISH FILLETS WITH A SHARP KNIFE TO NEATEN THEM INTO RECTANGULAR SHAPES. IF THE FILLETS ARE LARGE, CUT INTO RECTANGLES EACH ABOUT 7.5 X 10CM/3 X 4IN. WRAP TIGHTLY IN CLING FILM AND CHILL TO SET THE SHAPE. UNWRAP BEFORE COOKING.

with jus vanille

6 Melt another third of the butter in a medium pan and cook the fennel until nicely coloured. Add another ladleful of the vanilla stock to the pan along with the thyme and the bay leaf, cover and braise over a gentle heat for 8–10 minutes. Set aside.

7 When you are ready to cook the bass, preheat the oven to 200°C/400°F/Gas Mark 6. Remove the cling film if you have used it to wrap the fish fillets. Heat the oil in a heavy-based frying pan with heat-proof or removable handles – suitable for the oven.

8 Season the bass with salt, pepper and the remaining lemon juice. Add the last third of the butter to the pan. When it has stopped foaming, add the bass skin-side down. Cook for about 3-4 minutes, then flip the fillets over.

9 Transfer the pan to the oven to cook the flesh side of the fillets, also for 3-4 minutes. The flesh should feel just firm and lightly springy, and any liquid should have evaporated. Season the bass with My Special Pepper Mix (right).

10 To make the sauce, reheat the remaining vanilla stock and stir in the cream. Reheat the salsify bâtons and the fennel in their separate pans. Divide the fennel between each warmed plate. Put the fish on top, skin-side up. Arrange the salsify bâtons around the bass in a circle.

11 To finish the sauce, add the knob of ice-cold butter and reheat in the saucepan, frothing with a Bamix (see page 189 for supplier) or hand-held electric multi-blender. Spoon the frothy sauce over the fish and drizzle the remainder lightly over the salsify.

MY SPECIAL PEPPER MIX:

In a small bowl mix equal quantities of white and black peppercorns. Toss in some coriander seeds, 2-3 star anise and a few whole green cardamom pods. Funnel into a pepper mill and grind freshly whenever required.

Confit of tuna in red wine sauce

FRESH STEAKS OF TUNA ARE MEATY ENOUGH TO BE COOKED CONFIT-STYLE IN DUCK OR GOOSE FAT THEN SERVED WITH FULL-BODIED RED WINE SAUCE. THERE ARE MANY VARIETIES OF TUNA, BUT WE USE THE FRESHEST BLUE-FIN STEAKS FROM THE SOUTH OF FRANCE.

INGREDIENTS (for 4)

1 x quantity Red Wine Sauce (page 21)
4 x 180g/6oz fresh tuna steaks, skinned if necessary
500g/1lb 2oz new potatoes, scrubbed
85g/3oz/¾ stick butter
2 tablespoons olive oil
150g/5½oz baby onions, peeled
2 teaspoons icing sugar
200g/7oz fresh whole green beans, trimmed
300g/10oz asparagus tips, trimmed
2 teaspoons chopped parsley
500ml/18fl oz/2 cups duck or goose fat
sea salt and freshly ground black pepper

1 Have ready the Red Wine Sauce and set aside. Trim the tuna steaks into neat shapes if necessary.

2 Parboil the potatoes until almost cooked but still firm, then drain and cool. Cut into even slices for sautéeing; set aside.

3 Melt one-third of the butter in a heavy-based frying pan with half the oil and, when hot, sauté the onions, sprinkling over the icing sugar and stirring occasionally, for about 10 minutes or until caramelized and golden brown. Remove and keep warm.

4 Blanch the beans and asparagus separately in lightly salted boiling water until cooked but just firm. Drain and set aside in a warm place.

5 Heat the remaining butter and oil in a sauté pan and sauté the potatoes until golden brown and crisp, turning occasionally so they colour evenly. Drain, sprinkle with parsley and seasoning and keep warm. Meanwhile, reheat the Red Wine Sauce in a small saucepan and keep hot.

6 When you are ready to cook the tuna, heat the duck or goose fat in a deep-sided frying pan to a medium heat of about 65°C/160°F, or until a cube of day-old bread browns in about 1 minute.

7 Cook the tuna steaks, submerging them under the fat, for about 5-6 minutes. When cooked, they should be pale brown on the outside, nicely pink inside, and lightly springy to touch. Drain well on kitchen paper towels.

8 To serve, arrange a bed of potatoes in the centre of each warmed plate and place a tuna steak on top of each. Spoon the onions, beans and asparagus around the edge then spoon over the hot Red Wine Sauce and serve.

Dorade with pesto sauce

One of the Mediterranean fish traditionally associated with a classic bouillabaisse, dorade, or gilt-head bream, is also delicious served simply roasted or pan-fried, as in this recipe. Fine in texture, it is similar to sea bass and sometimes easier to find, although red or black bream make good substitutes if dorade is unobtainable. If filleting fish is not your forte, ask the fishmonger to do this for you.

INGREDIENTS (for 2)

1 whole dorade, about 800g/1lb 12oz filleted neatly in two
few sprigs thyme
about ¼ quantity Potato Purée (page 95)
2 tablespoons Pesto (page 19)
2-3 tablespoons Fish Stock (page 14)
8 baby globe artichokes
juice of ½ lemon
a little plain flour, for coating
about 3 tablespoons olive oil
1 clove garlic, peeled and crushed
2 medium scallops, shelled, trimmed and washed (page 40) then diced
2 tablespoons chopped chives
sprigs of tarragon
2 teaspoons chopped parsley
sea salt and freshly ground black pepper

1 Trim the dorade fillets neatly, then check for any fine pin bones and remove these with tweezers. Using the tip of a sharp knife, score the skin carefully a few times to prevent the fish from curling as it cooks. Pick the leaf 'flowers' off one of the thyme sprigs and scatter over the flesh. Cover and chill.

2 Have ready the Potato Purée, Pesto and Fish Stock. Reheat the Purée and keep warm. Thin down the Pesto with the Fish Stock and set aside.

3 Prepare the artichokes in the same way as for the Velouté of Artichokes with Fois Gras (step 2, page 47).

4 Place the flour in a bowl and season well. Drain the artichoke slices, pat dry and toss in the flour to coat lightly.

5 Heat a little of the oil in a non-stick frying pan and sauté the artichokes with the garlic until just tender. Season lightly then remove and keep warm.

6 Wipe the pan clean using kitchen paper towels and heat a little more of the oil until very hot, then quickly sauté the diced scallops until crisp; this should taken no more than 1 minute. Remove and keep warm.

7 Reheat the pan with the remaining oil. Season the dorade and then place skin-side down in the hot pan. Cook the fish for about 5 minutes or until almost done (it should be slightly springy and the skin crisp) then turn over and cook the flesh side for about 2 minutes.

8 To serve, heat the Pesto. Mix the chives into the Potato Purée and spoon onto the centre of each plate. Pour the Pesto around the potato and sprinkle the diced, fried scallops and artichoke slices over the sauce. Arrange the fish on top of the potato, garnish with sprigs of tarragon and thyme, and sprinkle over the chopped parsley.

Dorade with pesto sauce

Blanquette of turbot with oyster ravioli

A RECIPE THAT INSPIRED ME WHILE WORKING FOR PIERRE KOFFMAN AT LA TANTE CLAIRE. I LIKE THE MARRIAGE OF OYSTERS AND LITTLE CUCUMBER BALLS WITH THE MEATY TURBOT. IN THIS RECIPE FRESH PASTA IS USED IN TWO DIFFERENT WAYS, TO ENCLOSE AN OYSTER RAVIOLI AND FOR THE FRESH TAGLIATELLE, ALTHOUGH YOU COULD USE GOOD QUALITY READY-MADE TAGLIATELLE. FOR A SIMPLER DISH, THIS COULD BE MADE WITHOUT THE RAVIOLI.

INGREDIENTS (for 4)

200ml/7fl oz/⅞ cup Fish Stock (page 14)
¼ x quantity (140g/4½oz) homemade Pasta Dough (page 27) for the ravioli
250g/9oz homemade Tagliatelle (page 29) or fresh ready-made
350ml/12fl oz/1½ cups Fish Velouté (page 14)
1 large cucumber
200g/7oz young spinach leaves
4 large oysters, removed from their shells, juices reserved (page 36)
4 x 150g/5oz turbot fillets
25g/1oz/¼ stick butter
squeeze of lemon
1 heaped teaspoon each chopped chervil and chives
sea salt and ground white pepper

1 Have ready the Fish Stock, homemade Pasta Dough and Tagliatelle, if using, and the Fish Velouté and set aside.

2 Peel the cucumber then, using a very small melon baller, cut out as many cucumber balls as possible from the flesh, discarding the seeds. Blanch the balls in boiling water, drain and refresh in ice-cold water and set aside.

3 Blanch the spinach in lightly salted boiling water for about 1 minute, or until just wilted. Drain and refresh in cold water then drain again. Set aside.

4 For the ravioli, roll out the Pasta Dough and, using a 10cm/4in cutter, stamp out 8 circles to make 4 ravioli (steps 1-4, page 29). Blanch the oysters in a little simmering Fish Stock for just 30 seconds. Remove with a slotted spoon. Allow to cool, then use the oysters as a filling for the ravioli. Make sure the edges are well sealed. Blanch the ravioli in salted boiling water for about 1 minute then drain and keep warm.

5 Gently poach the turbot in the remaining Fish Stock for about 4-5 minutes or until it is about three-quarters cooked. Remove the fillets carefully with a slotted spoon and and keep warm. Boil the stock until syrupy and reduced by about two-thirds.

6 Stir in the Fish Velouté and return to the boil, cooking for about 2 minutes. Add the turbot fillets to this sauce and reheat for a further 2 minutes.

7 Cook the homemade Tagliatelle in boiling water for 30 seconds. If you are using ready-made, follow the pack instructions. Toss in half the butter and place in mounds in the centre of each plate. Reheat the cucumber and spinach separately in the remaining butter.

8 Place the turbot fillets on top of the Tagliatelle and sit a ravioli on top of that. Spoon the cucumber and spinach around the fish and pasta.

9 Reheat the Fish Velouté, season with lemon juice, salt and pepper, stirring in the herbs and any oyster juice just at the last moment. Pour the sauce over the ravioli and turbot and serve at once.

Roasted monkfish with boulangère potatoes

FIRM, MEATY MONKFISH TEAMS WELL WITH THE FRENCH COUNTRY STYLE OF THESE POTATOES, BAKED IN ROUNDS AND SERVED SIMPLY WITH FISH JUICES, A FRUITY OLIVE OIL AND LEMON JUICE. IDEALLY, YOU WILL NEED HOMEMADE STOCK FOR THIS RECIPE, BUT FAILING THAT YOU CAN SUBSTITUTE A VERY WEAK SOLUTION OF GOOD BOUILLON POWDER AND BOILING WATER.

INGREDIENTS (for 4)

4 x 300g/10oz monkfish fillets, skinned
softened butter, for greasing
olive oil for frying plus extra for greasing
a little plain flour, for coating
sea salt and freshly ground black pepper

FOR THE POTATOES:

250ml/9fl oz/1 cup Fish Stock (page 14) or Vegetable Nage (page 13)
4 medium potatoes, each weighing about 200g/7oz, peeled
2 cloves garlic, peeled and finely chopped
4 shallots, finely chopped
25g/1oz/¼ stick butter

TO SERVE:

juice of ½ lemon
a little olive oil
sprigs of tarragon and flat-leaf parsley

1 Have ready the Fish Stock or Vegetable Nage.

2 Make sure all the grey membrane is removed from the monkfish as this could cause the fish to curl and cook unevenly. If necessary, slice it off with a sharp, thin knife. Tear off 4 sheets of greaseproof paper large enough to make a parcel for each fillet. Brush the sheets lightly with softened butter.

3 Preheat the oven to 220°C/425°F/Gas Mark 7. Season the fillets then roll lightly in flour. Heat a little olive oil in a large frying pan and quickly seal the fish all over until just golden brown.

4 Wrap each fillet in a sheet of the paper, twisting the ends to seal. Place on a baking tray and transfer to the oven for 8-9 minutes.

5 While the fish is cooking, slice the potatoes thinly into rounds about 2mm/⅛in thick, using either a mandolin, the slicer blade of a food processor or a sharp knife. Place in a bowl, season well, then scatter the chopped garlic and shallots on top.

6 Cut 4 circles of greaseproof paper each 8cm/3¼in in diameter. Brush the circles with olive oil and place in a small, shallow roasting tin. Arrange the potato slices, together with the shallots and garlic, in overlapping slices on each paper circle.

7 Pour over the Fish Stock or Vegetable Nage and bring to a simmer on the top of the stove. Dot the potatoes with butter, then transfer the tin to the oven for around 10 minutes or until golden brown. When cooked, leave the slices in the stock.

8 Check the fish is cooked by pressing the thickest part of the fillet firmly with your finger. If it is firm and not at all springy then it is ready.

9 Allow the fish to stand in the paper for a few minutes while you slide the potatoes from their paper bases using a fish slice onto warm serving plates. Unwrap the fish, slice each fillet into 4-6 rounds and place on top of the potatoes. Trickle over any juices from the potato tin and from the fish parcels.

10 Sprinkle lemon juice and olive oil over the fish and potatoes, and garnish with the sprigs of tarragon and parsley.

Roasted monkfish with red wine sauce

MONKFISH IS A GOOD MEATY FISH AND CAN TAKE A FULL-FLAVOURED RED WINE SAUCE. WHY NOT? IT CERTAINLY WORKS WELL IN THE RESTAURANT. THE SAUCE CAN BE MADE IN ADVANCE AND THEN REHEATED, AS CAN THE SMALL AMOUNT OF RISOTTO THAT ACCOMPANIES IT.

INGREDIENTS (for 4)

1 x quantity Red Wine Sauce (page 21)
Shredded Leeks, to garnish (page 180)
4 x 150g/5oz monkfish fillets
½ teaspoon five-spice powder
1 tablespoon olive oil plus extra to serve

FOR THE RISOTTO:

200ml/7fl oz/⅞ cup Chicken Stock (page 18)
50g/2oz/¼ cup risotto rice e.g. Carnaroli, Arborio or Vialone Nano variety
2 tablespoons double cream
1 tablespoon mascarpone cheese
1 teaspoon each of chopped basil and chives

1 Have ready the Red Wine Sauce, Chicken Stock and Shredded Leeks and set aside.

2 Trim the monkfish fillets neatly, taking care to remove the grey membrane as this could cause the fish to curl if left on during cooking. Sprinkle with the five-spice powder and set aside in the refrigerator.

3 To make the risotto, simmer the rice in the Chicken Stock for about 12 minutes or until it is just soft, stirring occasionally. Season and set aside.

4 When you are ready to cook the monkfish, preheat the oven to 220°C/425°F/Gas Mark 7. Heat the oil in a heavy-based frying pan with heatproof or removable handles – suitable for the oven. Add the fillets and cook them for about 3 minutes on one side, then flip them over. Transfer the pan to the oven and cook for a further 5 minutes or so until just firm. Keep the fish warm.

5 To finish the risotto, gently reheat the rice and stir in the cream, mascarpone and herbs, then check the seasoning. Reheat the Red Wine Sauce.

6 Spoon the risotto into mounds in the centre of each warmed plate. Cut the monkfish into slices and arrange on top of the risotto.

7 Spoon the sauce around the fish then drizzle round the oil. Garnish with the Shredded Leeks and serve.

Roasted monkfish with red wine sauce

Bouillabaisse with saffron new potatoes

THIS CLASSIC MEDITERRANEAN FISH SOUP IS A JOY TO MAKE WHENEVER YOU CAN GET THE APPROPRIATE VARIETIES OF SEAFOOD. THE BOUILLABAISSE IS MADE IN TWO STAGES: FIRST THE BASE, FOR WHICH AN ASSORTMENT OF MEDITERRANEAN SEAFOOD IS COOKED AND PURÉED; SECOND, THE ADDITION OF CHUNKS OF FILLETED FISH SIMMERED WITH SAFFRON-SCENTED POTATOES. A BOUILLABAISSE IS NOT WORTH MAKING IN SMALL QUANTITIES SO IT IS IDEAL FOR ENTERTAINING. SERVE WITH ROUILLE (PAGE 21).

INGREDIENTS (for 12)

FOR THE BASIC BROTH:

3kg/6lb 10oz assorted Mediterranean seafood, choosen from at least 3 of the following: wrasse, perch, rascasse, sea bream, weever fish, large prawns, sea bass, red mullet and skinned fillets of conger eel

450ml/¾ pint/2¼ cups olive oil

2 large leeks, white parts only, sliced

400g/14oz onions, coarsely chopped

12 cloves garlic, unpeeled and crushed

800g/1lb 12oz very ripe tomatoes, roughly chopped

1 large Bouquet Garni (page 18)

2 bulbs fennel, roughly chopped

stalks of fresh basil, chervil and parsley

6 litres/10½ pints cold water

FOR THE GARNISH ADDITIONS:

2kg/4lb 8oz assorted fish, choosen from at least 3 of the following: John Dory, monkfish, sea bass, gurnard, red mullet and sea bream

1kg/2lb 4oz small new potatoes, left whole and scrubbed

2 large pinches of saffron strands

a little olive oil, to serve

2 tablespoons chopped chives

1 Begin by preparing the seafood: scale, cut and trim off fins. Keep heads intact but remove gills. Prawns can be left intact. If you obtain weever fish, have their poisonous spines removed when you buy them. To prepare the remaining fish for the garnish, scale, gut and trim them, removing the heads. Cut into bite-sized chunks.

2 To make the broth, heat the oil in a large saucepan or stockpot and add the leeks, onions, garlic, tomatoes, Bouquet Garni, fennel, herb stalks and fish. Sweat the ingredients over a low heat for about 20 minutes, stirring frequently.

3 Add the cold water, bring to the boil then simmer for 45-50 minutes. Remove from the heat and leave to stand for 20 minutes to allow the flavours to infuse.

4 Meanwhile, prepare the garnish of potatoes: parboil the potatoes with the saffron until half-cooked, then drain.

5 Pass the fish broth through a mouli food-mill or through a large sieve, rubbing with the back of a ladle. Discard the bones and other debris. Pour the broth through a fine sieve twice, again rubbing with a ladle. Check the seasoning.

6 To complete the Bouillabaisse, put the parboiled potatoes into a large casserole or saucepan then pour over the fish broth.

7 Bring to the boil then lower the heat to a slow simmer and cook for 5 minutes. Add the reserved chunks of fish for the garnish and a little trickle of olive oil and continue to cook for another 7-10 minutes, or until the fish is just firm and the potatoes soft.

8 Using a slotted spoon, gently lift out the fish and transfer to a large, warmed tureen. Pour over the broth and sprinkle over the chopped chives.

Bouillabaisse with

saffron new potatoes

Roasted brill with a brandade of cod

A BRANDADE IS A FLAKED FISH MIXTURE COMBINED WITH POTATO AND GARLIC. WE USE IT AS A BASE FOR SIMPLE 'ROASTED' FILLETS OF BRILL, SHARPENED WITH A SHALLOT AND SHERRY VINEGAR SAUCE. IF YOU LIKE, GARNISH WITH A TINY DISC OF POTATO RÖSTI. IF BRILL IS UNOBTAINABLE, YOU CAN USE FILLETS OF TURBOT OR JOHN DORY.

INGREDIENTS (for 4)

FOR THE BRANDADE:

1 tablespoon olive oil
200g/7oz cod fillets, skinned and cut into chunks
150g/5oz potatoes, peeled and diced
500ml/18fl oz/2 cups milk
1 clove garlic, peeled and crushed
2 tablespoons double cream
2 teaspoons chopped parsley

FOR THE SAUCE:

2 tablespoons Shallot Confit (page 94)
400ml/14fl oz/1¾ cups Veal Stock (page 16)
3 tablespoons Madeira
2 teaspoons sherry vinegar

FOR THE BRILL AND GARNISH:

200g/7oz young spinach leaves
25g/1oz/¼ stick butter
200g/7oz asparagus tips
2 x 300g/10½oz brill fillets, cut lengthways into 4 long fillets
2 tablespoons olive oil, plus extra for serving
Potato Rösti (page 94) (optional)
sea salt and freshly ground black pepper

1 Have ready the Shallot Confit and Veal Stock, and set aside.

2 For the brandade, heat a tablespoon of the oil in a heavy-based pan. 'Roast' the cod on the top of the stove until just cooked and golden. Remove, flake and cool.

3 Cook the potatoes in the milk along with the garlic and some salt and pepper until soft but not broken down. Drain through a colander set over a bowl, reserving the milk. Mash the potatoes in a large bowl until smooth, then slowly mix in the reserved milk and the cream, beating until you have a creamy paste. You may not need all the milk, but do use all the cream.

4 Using a spatula, fold the flaked cod gently into the potato, keeping the fish as flaky as possible. Season, mix in the parsley. and set aside.

5 To make the sauce, cook the Shallot Confit and Madeira in a small saucepan until the liquid is reduced by half. Deglaze with the sherry vinegar and cook again for a few seconds until reduced a little, then pour in the Veal Stock. Boil until reduced by half. Check the seasoning and set aside in a warm place.

6 Blanch the spinach in lightly salted boiling water until just wilted, drain, return to the pan, off the heat, with a little of the butter. Blanch the asparagus tips until just tender and return to their pan with the remaining butter.

7 To cook the brill, heat the oil in a heavy-based sauté pan set over a medium heat. Add the fillets, and cook for about 2 minutes on each side. Season well, remove and keep warm.

8 Reheat the brandade over a low heat in a saucepan. Arrange the spinach in a mound on each warmed plate. Place a fillet of brill on top of each mound. Reheat the asparagus if necessary and arrange around the edges. *Nappe* (coat) the fish with the sauce, trickling a little over the vegetables as well. Spoon one-quarter of the brandade on top of each fillet. Finally, dribble over a little olive oil and serve. If you like, garnish with a tiny Potato Rösti.

Roasted brill with

a brandade of cod

Fillets of John Dory with

Fillets of John Dory with pommes de terre écrasées

DURING THE EARLY SUMMER, WHEN JERSEY ROYAL POTATOES ARE AT THEIR BEST, IT IS GOOD TO CRUSH THEM AFTER COOKING WITH A MIXTURE OF OLIVE OIL, FRESH TOMATO AND GREEN HERBS. THIS IS ANOTHER IDEA I GAINED FROM MY TIME IN PARIS AND I FOUND IT MADE A WONDERFUL BASE FOR DELICATE DIAMONDS OF PAN-FRIED JOHN DORY, SERVED WITH A SWIRL OF FRESH TOMATO AND BALSAMIC VINEGAR CONCASSE. IT IS ALSO PARTICULARLY GOOD SERVED ON ITS OWN AS A SUMMER SALAD WITH A LIGHT MEDITERRANEAN TOUCH.

INGREDIENTS (for 4)

100g/3½oz Tomato Concasse (page 97) plus 4 teaspoons for the sauce
1 tablespoon Shallot Confit (page 94)
4 x 200g/7oz John Dory fillets, skinned
600g/1lb 5oz Jersey Royals or other fine baby new potatoes, washed and scrubbed
5 tablespoons olive oil
60g/2½oz/¼ cup pitted black olives, chopped
20g/¾oz chopped chives
1 tablespoon each of chopped basil, tarragon and coriander
juice of 1 lemon
sea salt and freshly ground black pepper

FOR THE SAUCE:

2 teaspoons Fresh Tomato Purée (page 97)
200ml/7fl oz/⅞ cup Vegetable Nage (page 13)
1 teaspoon balsamic vinegar
1 tablespoon chopped basil

1 Have ready the Tomato Concasse and Shallot Confit for the main dish, and the Fresh Tomato Purée and Vegetable Nage for the sauce. Set aside.
2 Cut each fish fillet into 3 long strips then cut these into 5cm/2in diamond shapes; set aside in the refrigerator.
3 Boil the potatoes in their skins for about 12 minutes or until just tender. Drain and leave for a few minutes until cool enough to handle. Peel while still warm and place in a large bowl.
4 Gently heat 2 tablespoons of the olive oil in a small saucepan then pour over the potatoes, crushing them lightly with a fork to form a chunky purée.
5 Mix in half the chopped olives, the Tomato Concasse, Shallot Confit, half the chopped chives, the other fresh herbs and the lemon juice. Season lightly, taking care as the olives will affect the seasoning. Cover and keep warm.
6 Put all the sauce ingredients, including the 4 teaspoons of Tomato Concasse and the remaining chopped chives and olives, into a small saucepan and set this aside until you are ready to heat and serve it.
7 Heat the remaining 3 tablespoons of olive oil in a large non-stick or well-seasoned frying pan. Fry the John Dory 'diamonds' for about 2-3 minutes or until just cooked and golden brown, turning once.
8 Using a scone cutter, about 6cm/2½in in diameter, press the potato mixture into rounds on warm dinner plates. Stack the fish on top, overlapping the pieces attractively.
9 Bring the sauce ingredients to the boil and spoon around each fish and potato mound. Serve at once.

pommes de terre écrasées

Escalope of salmon with sweet and sour pepper sauce

A DELICIOUS, LIGHT MAIN MEAL – CHICORY MAKES A FINE ACCOMPANIMENT TO THE FULL FLAVOUR OF SALMON AND LOOKS SPECTACULAR WHEN SERVED WITH THE VIBRANT COLOURS OF THE PEPPER SAUCE. ASK YOUR FISHMONGER TO CUT THE SALMON ESCALOPES FROM THE THICKEST END OF A SKINNED SALMON FILLET.

INGREDIENTS (for 4)

500ml/18fl oz/2 cups Vegetable Nage (page 13)
60g/2½oz/⅔ stick butter
2 red peppers, cored and finely chopped
2 yellow peppers, cored and finely chopped
6 shallots, finely chopped
1 sprig each of tarragon, chervil, basil and thyme
1 bay leaf
3 tablespoons Noilly Prat
1 teaspoon white wine vinegar
4 medium heads chicory
100g/4oz/½ cup caster sugar
4 x 200g/7oz salmon escalopes
sea salt and lemon juice

1 Have ready the Vegetable Nage and set aside.

2 Heat one-third of the butter in a medium saucepan and gently sweat the peppers and shallots with the herb sprigs and the bay leaf for about 10 minutes or until softened.

3 Stir in the Noilly Prat and cook uncovered until reduced down to about 1 tablespoon of glaze. Add the vinegar and about 150ml/¼ pint/⅔ cup of the Vegetable Nage. Simmer gently for about 20 minutes or until softened. Remove and discard the herbs; set aside.

4 Preheat the oven to 180°C/350°F/Gas Mark 4. Core the chicory heads carefully with a small, sharp knife and roll in the sugar.

5 Heat another third of the butter in a heavy-based frying pan with heatproof or removable handles – suitable for the oven. Add the heads of chicory and cook until they turn golden brown and caramelize. Pour over the remaining stock so that it half covers the chicory then transfer to the oven and cook for about 9 minutes or until the chicory is just tender. Set aside in a warm place.

6 Raise the oven setting to 200°C/400°F/Gas Mark 6. Place the salmon escalopes in a lightly greased pan or ovenproof dish and roast in the oven for about 10 minutes until pink and just firm.

7 To serve, reheat the sauce gently and whisk in the last of the butter. Reheat the chicory if necessary. Season the salmon to taste with salt and lemon juice, then arrange with the chicory on warmed plates and pour the sauce around. Serve immediately.

Escalope of salmon with

sweet and sour pepper sauce

Roasted baby lobster

Roasted baby lobster with jus citrus

A VISUAL TREAT, THIS DISH COMBINES DELICATE LOBSTER WITH A TWIST OF CITRUS SEGMENTS, AND YOU DON'T NEED PERFECTLY SHAPED LOBSTERS.

INGREDIENTS (for 2)

Court-bouillon (page 16) or salted water, for poaching

100g/3½oz homemade Tagliatelle (page 29) or fresh ready-made

2 live baby lobsters, each weighing about 400-500g/14-16oz

200g/7oz young asparagus tips

12 baby leeks, whole, or 6 small, thin ones, halved

40g/1½oz/⅓ stick butter

2 tablespoons olive oil

FOR THE JUS CITRUS:

200ml/7fl oz/⅞ cup Vegetable Nage (page 13)

1 x quantity Candied Orange Peel (page 187) (optional)

1 pink grapefruit

1 orange

1 lemon

1 lime

1 tablespoon chopped chervil

4 basil leaves, cut into fine julienne strips

sea salt and ground white pepper

1 Have ready the Court-bouillon (if using), the Vegetable Nage, the home-made Tagliatelle and the Candied Orange Peel (if using) and set aside.

2 To kill the lobsters, lay each one on a board stomach downwards, then pierce firmly through the cross mark on its skull with the tip of a large sharp knife. Pour Court-bouillon or salted water into a large saucepan, allowing just enough to cover the lobsters. Bring to the boil.

3 Plunge the lobsters into the simmering water and cook for 1 minute. Remove, allow to cool until comfortable enough to handle with a tea towel, then slice each lobster in half lengthways through the stomach shell and open it out flat. Cut off the claws. Remove the meat carefully from the tail and claws. Discard the entrails and shells but reserve the heads for the garnish, if liked. Place the lobster meat in the refrigerator to firm up.

4 Meanwhile, make the sauce: cut the peel and pith from the citrus fruits, then cut four segments each from the grapefruit and orange, and two each from the lemon and lime. Work over a bowl to catch the juices. Squeeze the unsegmented parts of the fruits for their juice and combine with the saved juices.

5 Boil the Vegetable Nage until reduced by half. Add 2 tablespoons of the citrus juices and simmer for a further 2-3 minutes. Gently whisk in the fruit segments until they dissolve into tiny cells. Set aside and keep warm.

6 Cook the asparagus tips and leeks together in salted water until just tender, then drain and return to the pan with one-third of the butter to glaze. Pour in a little of the leftover citrus juice for flavour. Boil and drain the Tagliatelle, glaze with another third of the butter and keep warm.

7 Heat the oil in a large, non-stick pan. Season the lobster meat then 'roast' the tail meat on the top of the stove for about 6-8 minutes, adding the claw meat halfway through. Turn frequently to caramelize the flesh evenly.

8 To serve, roll the Tagliatelle into a spiral around a fork and place in the centre of a warm plate. Slice the tail meat and place over the pasta, then arrange the claw meat to each side. Garnish with the asparagus and leeks. Reheat the sauce and whisk in the remaining butter. Stir in the chervil, check the seasoning and coat the lobster. Garnish with basil and Candied Orange Peel if using.

with jus citrus

Meat, game and poultry

Our best sales of meat and poultry are in the autumn and winter when our customers prefer a more substantial main course. Game is a great favourite too because its short season gives such a burst of excitement, especially venison, which comes from Scotland and is hung to a dark ruby red. We serve medallions of saddle meat with an exotic dark chocolate and raspberry vinegar sauce.

Our beef is from Scotland, too, and is only admitted into my kitchens after it has been hung for at least three and a half weeks. Fillet of beef and oxtail are our favourite cuts – the former for a light pan-roasting, the latter for cooking long and lovingly until the meat falls easily from the bone for shredding and wrapping in crépinettes.

Offal, too, is a personal favourite and a challenge, tempting me into an adventurous mood which might result in my dusting sweetbreads with curry powder and serving them with a Sauternes sauce. Duck foie gras, a somewhat unique form of offal, we use melted into sauces – wonderful with chicken!

Our birds (chicken and pigeon) come from Bresse in France. These I cook in the poché-grillé *way, part poaching to moisten, then roasting to render down the fat and to crisp and flavour the skin.*

Fillet of beef with braised oxtail

THIS MAJESTIC RECIPE HAS A NUMBER OF DIFFERENT ELEMENTS: PERFECTLY SHAPED SLICES OF FILLET OF BEEF NESTLING ON SPINACH AND A CRISP POTATO RÖSTI, A BRIGHT LAYER OF CREAMED PARSLEY, VEGETABLE GARNISHES AND AN UNUSUAL ACCOMPANIMENT OF *CRÉPINETTE* OF BRAISED OXTAIL. THAT'S NOT ALL: THE WHOLE DISH IS ENHANCED WITH A RICH RED WINE SAUCE THAT HAS THE DISTINCTION OF BEING LIGHT YET FULL FLAVOURED.

THE SECRET TO THIS SAUCE IS TWO-FOLD: FIRST, I REDUCE A WHOLE BOTTLE OF WINE RIGHT DOWN UNTIL IT IS DEEP AND SYRUPY AND, SECOND, I USE A COMBINATION OF TWO STOCKS – CHICKEN AND VEAL – RATHER THAN ONE. I FIND IF THAT VEAL STOCK IS USED ON ITS OWN, THE RESULTANT SAUCE IS TOO STICKY. YOU WILL NEED TO START THIS RECIPE ABOUT 1½ DAYS IN ADVANCE, BUT DON'T BE PUT OFF. MOST OF THE ELEMENTS CAN BE MADE AHEAD THEN PULLED TOGETHER IN TRIUMPH! ALTERNATIVELY, YOU COULD SIMPLIFY THIS RECIPE BY SERVING THE STEAK WITHOUT THE OXTAIL, AND OFFERING AS ACCOMPANIMENTS POTATO PURÉE (PAGE 95) AND CREAMED PARSLEY.

INGREDIENTS (for 4)

FOR THE BRAISED OXTAIL:

1 whole oxtail, about 1kg/2lb 4oz in weight, chopped in pieces
½ x 75cl bottle good red wine
1 sprig thyme
1 bay leaf
about 5 tablespoons olive oil
2 carrots, coarsely chopped
1 onion, coarsely chopped
1 litre/1¾ pints/4½ cups Veal Stock (page 16)
caul fat (see Glossary, page 188)
sea salt and freshly ground black pepper

FOR THE RED WINE SAUCE:

500ml/18fl oz/2 cups Chicken Stock (page 18)
500ml/18fl oz/2 cups Veal Stock (page 16)
1 x 75cl bottle good red wine
about 2 tablespoons olive oil
8 shallots, sliced
beef trimmings taken from the fillet of beef
12 black peppercorns
1 sprig thyme
1 small bay leaf
1 tablespoon sherry vinegar

FOR THE FILLET OF BEEF:

1 whole fillet of beef, weighing about 600g/1lb 5oz
1 tablespoon olive oil
15g/½oz/1 tablespoon butter

1 About 1½ days before you intend serving the dish, marinate the oxtail: put the pieces into a bowl and cover with the half-bottle of red wine. Add the sprig of thyme and the bay leaf. Cover the surface with cling film, fitting it around the oxtail rather than the rim of the bowl and holding the meat in place beneath the wine with a weight. This will ensure the oxtail takes on a good rich colour. Transfer to the refrigerator to marinate for 24 hours.

2 Trim the fillet of the side 'chain' and tail end so that you have a neat roll. You may need to remove the shiny sinew as well, or ask the butcher to do this. Wrap the fillet tightly in cling film and chill overnight. This helps keep it round. Chop the trimmings roughly and set aside separately.

3 Have ready the Chicken and Veal Stocks. Prepare, and set aside, the Glazed Baby Onions and the Creamed Parsley.

4 Next make the Red Wine Sauce. Boil down the bottle of red wine until reduced to about 100ml/3½fl oz/½ cup. Meanwhile, in a separate saucepan, ▶

Fillet of beef with braised oxtail

heat 2 tablespoons of oil and sauté the shallots, the reserved beef trimmings and the peppercorns, thyme and bay leaf, until the shallots are nice and caramelized. Deglaze the pan with the sherry vinegar, stirring until evaporated.

5 Pour in the reduced red wine 'syrup', all of the Chicken Stock and one-third of the Veal Stock. Bring to the boil then simmer for about 20 minutes or until reduced by one-third, skimming a few times in between with a ladle to remove any scum.

6 Pour through a sieve lined with wet muslin or a clean tea towel at least twice to remove all the particles. Check the seasoning and set aside.

7 When the oxtail has marinated sufficiently, remove it from its marinade and pat dry with kitchen paper towels. Reserve the marinade.

8 In an ovenproof saucepan (e.g. of cast iron), heat about 3 tablespoons of the oil and, when very hot, add the oxtail pieces and brown them all over – in fact until they are almost blackened and well caramelized. This process helps the flavour to develop. Remove the oxtail pieces and wipe out the pan with kitchen paper towels.

9 Add the remaining 2 tablespoons of oil to the pan and sweat the carrots and onions until softened. Add the reserved marinade and the Veal Stock and boil down to reduce by half to concentrate the flavour.

10 Preheat the oven to 180°C/350°F/Gas Mark 4. Place the oxtail in the pan with the vegetables and reduced stock. Cover and braise in the oven for 2½–3 hours or until the meat is meltingly tender and starts to leave the bone.

11 With a slotted spoon, remove the oxtail and transfer to a dish. Reserve the braising liquor. When the meat is cool enough to handle, pull it into fine shreds and discard any fat, gristle and bones.

12 Strain the braising liquor through a sieve set over a bowl. Discard the vegetables. Return the braising liquor to the pan and set it over high heat on the top of the stove. Boil down the liquor until it becomes very syrupy, and has reduced to about 300ml/½ pint/1¼ cups. This will be the binding agent for the oxtail shreds. Check the seasoning, then gradually add just enough of the reduced liquor, a small amount at a time, to the shreds so that they bind together. Make sure the mixture is only just bound and not too wet. You should have about one-third of the reduced liquor left for reheating later.

13 Chill the bound oxtail mixture until firm, then divide it into four round balls ready to be wrapped in caul fat. In the restaurant we sometimes divide the mixture into a larger number of baby *crépinettes* for each serving but the wrapping process is quite time-consuming. Alternatively, if you don't intend to use caul fat, shape the mixture into 4 little patties.

TO GARNISH:

24 Glazed Baby Onions (page 93)
½ x quantity Creamed Parsley (page 100)
4 Potato Rösti (page 94)
15g/½oz/1 tablespoon butter
100g/3½oz wild or brown mushrooms of your choice
100g/3½oz young spinach leaves
2 tablespoons double cream

14 If you are going to use caul fat, soak it in cold water to remove any traces of blood. Unravel it gently to avoid tears then pat it dry. Take an oxtail ball and wrap it in a piece of caul fat large enough to contain it with some overlap. Twist the overlapping caul fat tightly underneath the ball. Repeat with the remaining oxtail balls. Leftover caul fat can be frozen for use in another recipe.

15 Prepare the Potato Rösti for the garnish, and set aside, uncovered, in a warm place. They will remain crisp.

16 Reheat the Glazed Baby Onions and the Creamed Parsley, making sure the latter is light and creamy. Reheat the Red Wine Sauce.

17 In a sauté pan, heat half the butter for the garnish until it just stops foaming and quickly sauté the mushrooms until lightly cooked. Set aside and keep warm.

18 Blanch the spinach leaves for about 1 minute or until just wilted, then drain and squeeze dry in a clean tea towel. Reheat in a small pan with the cream then season to taste.

19 Reheat the reserved oxtail braising liquor. It should have a syrupy consistency. If it looks too thick, then let it down with a little stock. Simmer the oxtail *crépinettes* in this liquor for about 5 minutes, stirring lightly in the pan. Remove the *crépinettes* with a slotted spoon and take off the caul fat leaving a lacy pattern. This is a process we always do in the Aubergine for a special touch, but you can leave the caul fat on if you prefer.

20 You are now ready to pull all the elements together for serving. Remove the wrapped fillet of beef from the refrigerator and take off the cling film. Cut the fillet across into four equal-size rounds of steak. Heat a tablespoon of oil in a heavy-based frying pan, add 15g/½oz/1 tablespoon butter and, when it starts to foam, add the steaks and pan-fry them according to taste. In the restaurant we prefer them to be medium cooked (right).

21 Place each Potato Rösti on a small mound of creamed spinach in the centre of each large warmed plate. Put a steak on each Potato Rösti, shape the Creamed Parsley into quenelles (page 173) and place one on each steak. Arrange the oxtail *crépinette,* the Glazed Baby Onions and sautéed mushrooms around the steak. Drizzle the Red Wine Sauce over the steak, vegetables and the oxtail to glaze. Serve in triumph!

COOKING STEAKS – THE FINGER TIP TEST

WHEN ASKED HOW LONG I LEAVE STEAKS TO COOK, I REPLY WITH THIS HINT: CHECK BY PRESSING THE TOP OF THE STEAK WITH YOUR FINGER TIPS. TIMINGS DEPEND ON THE THICKNESS OF THE STEAK AND WHETHER IT NEEDS TO BE VERY RARE OR MEDIUM. WITH RARE STEAKS, YOUR FINGERS SHOULD ALMOST SINK INTO THE STEAK WITH VIRTUALLY NO BOUNCE AS IT COOKS. MEDIUM STEAKS WILL HAVE A SLIGHT COMEBACK AND BE A LITTLE BOUNCY. MEDIUM TO WELL-DONE STEAKS WILL FEEL FIRMER BUT STILL HAVE A LITTLE SPRING. WELL-DONE STEAKS – NO COMMENT!

Venison with

Venison with chocolate sauce

FARMED VENISON IS ONE OF THE UNSUNG SUCCESS STORIES OF MODERN ANIMAL HUSBANDRY. IT IS LEAN, TENDER MEAT, NATURALLY REARED AND ALSO LOW IN SATURATED FAT. BECAUSE VENISON IS A FULL-FLAVOURED MEAT IT WILL SUPPORT AN ASSERTIVE SAUCE, WHICH IN THIS CASE IS A COMBINATION OF THE OLD AND THE NEW WORLD: RED WINE, RASPBERRY VINEGAR AND VEAL STOCK REDUCED RIGHT DOWN AND FLAVOURED IN THE ORIGINAL AZTEC FASHION WITH DARK, BITTER CHOCOLATE.

1 To make the sauce, have ready the Veal Stock. Using a large saucepan, sauté the shallots and garlic in the 25g/1oz/¼ stick of butter, along with the thyme, bay leaf and peppercorns, until nicely caramelized and softened.

2 Deglaze with the raspberry vinegar then pour in the wine and boil until it has reduced to about 100ml/3½fl oz/½ cup and is syrupy in consistency.

3 Add the Veal Stock and boil until reduced by three-quarters to about 600ml/1 pint/2½ cups. Pour the sauce through a fine sieve set over a bowl, rubbing gently with the back of a ladle. Return the sauce to the pan. Stir in the chocolate until it melts, reheating very gently if necessary, but taking care not to let the sauce boil. Check the seasoning.

4 To prepare the vegetables, in another saucepan gently sauté the carrots, celeriac and bacon in the 50g/2oz/½ stick of butter until golden brown. Place half of this mixture in a separate pan and set aside. Add the cabbage to the original pan and continue cooking for a further 3-4 minutes.

5 Drain the butter from the cabbage mixture and add the cream. Boil briskly to reduce by half until lightly thickened. Check the seasoning and set aside.

6 Preheat the oven to 220°C/425°F/Gas Mark 7. Season the venison steaks. Heat the oil in an ovenproof sauté pan and brown the steaks until well sealed all over – about 3 minutes. Cover with a butter paper or sheet of buttered greaseproof paper and roast in the oven for 4-5 minutes. Remove and set aside to rest. At this stage the venison should be slightly pink inside.

7 Reheat the cabbage mixture and the reserved uncreamed vegetables separately. Gently reheat the sauce, being careful not to let it boil or it will separate.

8 Spoon the cabbage mixture onto warmed plates. Slice the venison steaks and arrange these on top. Arrange the remaining vegetables around the meat. *Nappe* (coat) the meat and vegetables with sauce and serve.

INGREDIENTS (for 4)

400g/14oz carrot, cut into 1cm/½in dice
400g/14oz celeriac, cut into 1cm/½in dice
300g/10oz smoked bacon, cut into 1cm/½in dice
50g/2oz/½ stick butter
½ small Savoy cabbage, cut into thin julienne strips
200ml/7fl oz/⅞ cup double cream
4 x 150g/5oz fillet of venison steaks, trimmed
1 tablespoon olive oil
sea salt and freshly ground black pepper

FOR THE SAUCE:

2 litres/3½ pints/9 cups Veal Stock (page 16)
500g/1lb 2oz shallots, coarsely chopped
4 cloves garlic, unpeeled and crushed
25g/1oz/¼ stick butter
2 sprigs thyme
1 bay leaf
2 teaspoons black peppercorns
2 teaspoons raspberry vinegar
1 x 75cl bottle red wine
40g/1½oz dark, bitter chocolate, broken into small pieces

chocolate sauce

Caramelized calf's sweetbreads with jus Sauternes

A POPULAR CHOICE AT THE AUBERGINE BUT RARELY EATEN AT THE DOMESTIC TABLE, SWEETBREADS ARE SIMPLE TO PREPARE AT HOME. USE ONLY SWEETBREADS FROM THE PANCREAS GLAND, SOMETIMES KNOWN AS THE HEARTBREADS. THERE IS NO NEED TO BLANCH THEM, ALTHOUGH THIS IS OFTEN RECOMMENDED FOR SUPPOSED EASIER SKINNING: A SHARP FILLETING KNIFE IS JUST AS EFFECTIVE.

INGREDIENTS (FOR 4)

4 x 150g/5½oz calf's sweetbreads (2 pairs)
2 tablespoons olive oil
1 teaspoon mild curry powder
1 teaspoon sea salt
200g/7oz carrots, cut into thin bâtons or julienne strips
100g/3½oz/1 stick unsalted butter
200g/7oz young spinach leaves
about 24 shallots, peeled
75g/3oz girolles

FOR THE SAUCE:

75ml/2½fl oz/⅓ cup 2 tablespoons Chicken Stock (page 18), plus 1 tablespoon for the spinach
75ml/2½fl oz/⅓ cup 2 tablespoons Sauternes or other sweet white wine
25g/1oz/¼ stick unsalted butter, chilled and diced
sea salt and freshly ground black pepper

1 To make the sauce, have ready the Chicken Stock. Pour the Sauternes into a small saucepan and boil down until reduced by half. Add the Chicken Stock and boil down again to reduce by half.

2 Using a thin, sharp filleting knife, remove the membrane from the sweetbreads, sliding the knife under the membrane and working the knife away from you in a sawing action. Preheat the oven to 200°C/400°F/Gas Mark 6.

3 Heat the oil in a heavy-based frying pan over a medium heat and brown the sweetbreads for about 4-5 minutes on each side, or until caramelized and golden brown. Sprinkle over the curry powder and salt while cooking.

4 Remove from the heat, cover each sweetbread with a butter paper or buttered greaseproof paper and transfer to the oven. Cook for about 8 minutes or until firm. Remove and set aside in a warm place, still covered.

5 Cook the carrots with one-quarter of the 100g/3½oz/1 stick butter and enough water to barely cover them until just cooked and firm – about 5 minutes. The water should have almost evaporated. Season, and keep warm.

6 Cook the spinach in another quarter of the butter and 1 tablespoon of Chicken Stock or water, until just wilted. Drain, season and keep warm.

7 In a heavy-based pan, cook the shallots gently in another quarter of the butter, turning frequently until soft and golden brown. Remove and drain.

8 Add the remaining quarter of the butter to the same pan and sauté the girolles for a few minutes until just softened. Remove and drain.

9 To finish the sauce, reheat until just boiling. Taste for seasoning and whisk in the 25g/1oz/¼ stick of chilled and diced butter.

10 Squeeze dry the spinach in a clean tea towel and place a mound in the centre of each warmed plate. Arrange a sweetbread on top of each then crown with the carrots. Place the shallots and girolles around the sweetbreads. Reheat the sauce and whisk to a froth with a Bamix (see page 189 for supplier) or a hand-held electric multi-blender. Pour around the sweetbreads.

Caramelized calf's sweetbreads

with jus Sauternes

Rump of

Rump of lamb Niçoise

NIÇOISE DISHES ARE BRIGHT AND COLOURFUL WITH STRONG, GUTSY FLAVOURS OF PEPPERS, GARLIC, TOMATOES AND OLIVES. COMBINE SUCH ELEMENTS WITH PLUMP LAMB ROASTED UNTIL IT IS JUST TENDER AND YOU HAVE A DISH THAT TRULY REFLECTS THE VIBRANCY OF PROVENCE. FOR RUMPS OF LAMB, ASK YOUR BUTCHER TO CUT THICK BONELESS CUTLETS FROM THE END OF A SADDLE OF LAMB WHERE IT JOINS THE LEG.

INGREDIENTS (for 4)

700ml/1¼ pints/3 cups Lamb Stock (page 17)
2 teaspoons each of chopped basil and tarragon
4 boneless rumps of lamb each weighing about 250g/9oz
40g/1½oz/⅓ stick melted clarified butter or 2 tablespoons olive oil
100g/3½oz/½ cup black olives, pitted and halved
sea salt and freshly ground black pepper

FOR THE NIÇOISE GARNISH:

4 x Potato Rösti (page 94)
24 x Candied Aubergine Slices (page 180)
24 x Glazed Baby Onions (page 93)
2 courgettes
4 ripe tomatoes
2 large sprigs each of thyme and rosemary
100ml/3½fl oz/½ cup olive oil

1 Have ready the Lamb Stock, Potato Rösti, Glazed Baby Onions and Candied Aubergine Slices.

2 To prepare the Niçoise garnish, cut the courgettes into 1cm/½in thick slices. Dip the tomatoes briefly in boiling water, skin, deseed and cut them into quarters. Pick off the tips of the sprig of thyme to form little 'flowers' and chop the rosemary.

3 Add the oil to a medium saucepan and lightly sauté the courgettes along with the thyme 'flowers' and chopped rosemary for about 6 minutes or until just softened. Remove with a slotted spoon and drain on kitchen paper towels. Sauté the tomato quarters until just softened, remove and drain. Season the sautéed vegetables and set aside together in a warm place.

4 To make the sauce, boil down the Lamb Stock by about two-thirds. Stir in the chopped basil and tarragon. Check the seasoning.

5 To cook the lamb, first preheat the oven to 190°C/375°F/Gas Mark 5. Heat the clarified butter or oil in a cast-iron frying pan and brown the lamb joints all over. Transfer the pan to the oven and roast for 8–10 minutes. Remove the meat, season it and leave to rest, covered in a warm place, for about 5 minutes.

6 Slice the rumps thinly. Place a Potato Rösti in the centre of each warmed plate and arrange slices of lamb on each. Distribute the sautéed vegetables, the Glazed Baby Onions, the halved olives and the Candied Aubergine Slices around them. Spoon the sauce over the lamb and vegetables and serve.

lamb Niçoise

Roast best end of lamb with Puy lentils

LAMB IS ALWAYS A POPULAR CHOICE ON OUR MENU, AND THIS IS A PRETTY DISH FOR LATE SPRING WHEN NEW LAMB IS AT ITS BEST. I TAKE WELL-TRIMMED FILLETS FROM THE BEST END OF THE LAMB AND ROLL THEM IN CHOPPED FRESH HERBS BEFORE ROASTING AND SLICING.

INGREDIENTS (for 2)

300ml/½ pint/1¼ cups Lamb Stock (page 17)
2 x Potato Rösti (page 94)
½ x quantity Glazed Baby Onions (page 93)
100g/3½oz Tomato Concasse (page 97)
50g/2oz/⅓ cup Puy lentils, soaked overnight
1 Bouquet Garni (page 18)
1 small onion, peeled and halved
1 small carrot, peeled
40g/1½oz/⅓ stick butter
50g/2oz Savoy cabbage, cut into fine julienne strips
about 8 small asparagus spears
1 whole best end of lamb
1 teaspoon each of finely chopped chervil, basil, chives and parsley
1 tablespoon olive oil
sea salt and freshly ground black pepper

1 Have ready the Lamb Stock, Potato Rösti, Glazed Baby Onions and Tomato Concasse. Boil the Lamb Stock until reduced by two-thirds. Set aside.
2 Drain the lentils, then place in a saucepan with the Bouquet Garni, onion and carrot. Cover with fresh water, bring to the boil, then turn down to a simmer and cook for about 15-20 minutes until just tender. Drain, remove the Bouquet Garni, onion and carrot then set aside.
3 In a small pan, melt half the butter and sweat the cabbage for 2 minutes or until just wilted, stirring occasionally. Mix with the lentils and set aside.
4 Blanch the asparagus in a little boiling water for 2 minutes, then drain, refresh in cold water, drain again and set aside.
5 Preheat the oven to 200°C/400°F/Gas Mark 6. Cut the meat from both sides of the best end of lamb and trim into neat fillets (we call these cannons). Mix together the herbs, setting aside about 2 teaspoons for the sauce. Roll the cannons in the remaining herbs, making sure they are evenly coated.
6 Heat the oil in an ovenproof sauté pan and fry the cannons quickly on all sides to seal, then cover the meat with a butter paper or some buttered greaseproof paper. Roast in the oven for 5-6 minutes or until the cannons are just pink in the centre. Remove and set aside without removing the paper.
7 Reheat the Potato Rösti in the oven and the Glazed Baby Onions in a pan (they won't need additional liquid). Return the Lamb Stock to the boil, add the reserved herbs, check seasoning and whisk in half the remaining butter.
8 Using the last of the butter, reheat the lentils and cabbage in one pan and the asparagus in another. Place a 7.5cm/3in cutter in the centre of each warm plate and spoon in the lentil and cabbage mixture, patting down lightly. Remove the cutters and place a Potato Rösti on top of each mound.
9 Cut the lamb into neat slices and place on the Rösti. Arrange the Glazed Baby Onions, Tomato Concasse and asparagus around the lentils and lamb. Bring the sauce just back to the boil, *nappe* (coat) the lamb with about a spoonful and spoon the rest over the vegetables. Serve immediately.

Roast best end of

lamb with Puy lentils

Roast rump of veal with sautéed cèpes

A SIMPLE, PAN-ROASTED DISH OF A JUICY RUMP OF VEAL, SLICED INTO MEDALLIONS AND SERVED WITH SAUTÉED CÈPES AND LIGHT VEAL JUS. ASK YOUR BUTCHER FOR A PIECE OF VEAL TOP RUMP, WHICH IS A ROASTING CUT SIMILAR TO BEEF TOP RUMP, THEN CUT IT INTO TWO LONG PIECES AND USE KITCHEN STRING TO TIE EACH INTO NEAT ROLLS.

INGREDIENTS (for 4)

2 tablespoons Shallot Confit (page 94)
1 tablespoon Tomato Concasse (page 97)
200ml/7fl oz/⅞ cup Veal Stock (page 16)
4 Potato Rösti (page 94)
800g/1lb 12oz top rump of veal
200g/7oz fresh cèpes or other wild mushrooms, sliced
3 tablespoons olive oil
2 teaspoons chopped chives
200g/7oz young spinach leaves
25g/1oz/¼ stick butter
4 tablespoons ruby port
sea salt and freshly ground black pepper

1 Have ready the Shallot Confit, Tomato Concasse, Veal Stock and the Potato Rösti, and set aside.

2 Trim the meat of any fat and cut it lengthways into 2 strips, each very approximately 15cm/6in long. Tie each of these into long fillet shapes, tightening the string to neaten into a roll. Preheat the oven to 220°C/425°F/Gas Mark 7.

3 Sauté the cèpes or mushrooms in 2 tablespoons of the oil for about 5 minutes or until just softened. Stir in the Shallot Confit, the Tomato Concasse and the chives. Season and set aside in a warm place.

4 Blanch the spinach in a little boiling water with half the butter, then drain well and keep warm.

5 Season the veal rolls and place on a roasting tin. Brush with the remaining oil. Roast for 10–12 minutes or until lightly springy to the touch and just pink in the centre.

6 To make the sauce of veal jus, bring the Veal Stock to the boil together with the port. Boil until reduced by one-third then check the seasoning. Whisk in the remaining butter.

7 Arrange the spinach in a mound in the centre of each warmed plate, then place a Potato Rösti on top of each.

8 Untie the veal rolls and slice each into about 5–6 medallions. Place these on top of each Rösti then arrange the garnish of sautéed cèpes and Tomato Concasse around the edge.

9 Spoon a little of the sauce over the veal then trickle the remainder over the garnish. Serve hot.

Poulet Bresse *poché-grillé* with sauce foie gras

THIS STYLE OF HALF POACHING AND HALF GRILLING POULTRY IS OFTEN USED FOR COOKING PIGEON IN FRANCE. HERE I HAVE ADAPTED IT TO SUIT CHICKEN. THE METHOD COMBINES POACHING THE FLESH ON THE BONE, WHICH KEEPS THE MEAT MOIST, WITH GRILLING, WHICH HELPS TO RELEASE THE FAT SO THAT THE MEAT IS JUST TENDER AND THE SKIN CRISPY. FOR ME, THE BEST CHICKEN IS THE FRENCH POULET BRESSE WITH ITS CHARACTERISTIC BLACK LEGS AND FINE FLESH. POULET BRESSE BIRDS CAN BE FOUND IN CERTAIN SPECIALITY BUTCHERS, BUT YOU COULD USE A GOOD FREE-RANGE BIRD. THE CAPPUCCINO-STYLE SAUCE CAN BE SERVED AS IT IS, OR, FOR TRUE AUBERGINE STYLE, SKIM THE FROTH ONLY AND SPOON OVER THE BREASTS.

INGREDIENTS (for 4)

2 small Poulet Bresse or free-range chickens, each weighing about 900g-1kg/2-2¼lb
250g/9oz homemade Tagliatelle (page 29) or fresh ready-made
50g/2oz/½ stick butter plus an extra knob for finishing
2 tablespoons olive oil
375g/13oz baby onions or shallots, peeled
300g/10oz baby spinach leaves
100g/3½oz petits pois
100g/3½oz baby broad beans, unpodded
2 sprigs tarragon

FOR THE SAUCE:

2.5 litres/4½pints Chicken Stock (page 18)
1 bay leaf
1 sprig rosemary
1 carrot, roughly chopped
½ medium onion, roughly chopped
½ celery stick, roughly chopped
6 white peppercorns
200g/7oz fresh foie gras
150ml/¼pint/¾ cup double cream
25g/1oz/¼ stick unsalted butter
squeeze of lemon juice
sea salt and freshly ground black pepper

1 Have ready the Chicken Stock and set aside.

2 Cut off the legs and wings from the Poulet Bresse or free-range chickens. These can be used for another dish, perhaps in a mid-week casserole. Leave the breasts intact on the carcass of each chicken.

3 If you are using homemade Tagliatelle, blanch for one minute, drain and set aside. For fresh ready-made, follow the pack instructions.

4 Heat the butter and half the oil in a sauté pan and gently fry the onions or shallots until lightly browned, shaking the pan occasionally. Remove from the pan and set aside.

5 Blanch the spinach in a minimum of water, just enough to cover, for a few seconds until wilted, then drain in a sieve and refresh under cold water to arrest cooking and preserve the colour. Squeeze gently in a clean tea towel or kitchen paper towels to dry. Set aside.

6 Blanch the petits pois and the unpodded broad beans in separate pans in salted boiling water. Drain. Pod the broad beans and set aside both peas and beans in a warm place.

7 Now make the sauce. Preheat the oven to its lowest temperature. In a large saucepan, put the Chicken Stock to boil along with the bay leaf, rosemary, carrot, onion, celery and peppercorns. Add the birds, ensuring the breasts are submerged in the stock.

8 Turn the heat down so the liquid is at a very gentle simmer, with just the occasional bubble, then cover and poach the birds for 10 minutes. Remove them, cover loosely in foil, and keep warm in the oven.

9 Return the poaching stock to the heat and boil rapidly until reduced by about half. Strain through a fine sieve and reserve about 400ml/14fl oz/1¾ cups. The remaining stock can be used in another recipe or frozen. ▶

10 Off the heat, add the foie gras in pieces to the reserved stock, stirring until smooth. Mix in the cream and butter. Add a squeeze or two of fresh lemon juice and season to taste. Heat until just on the point of boiling then remove from the heat and set aside.

11 Meanwhile, preheat the grill until hot. Remove the birds from the oven, unwrap them and cut the half-poached breasts from each carcass, retaining the skin. Grill the breasts skin-side up for about 4 minutes then, with a sharp knife, slash each breast diagonally a few times, wrap loosely in foil and return to the oven to keep warm.

12 Heat the remaining oil in a pan and briefly fry the tarragon leaves, being careful not to burn them. Drain and set aside.

13 Heat a knob of butter in a sauté pan and quickly reheat the Tagliatelle, the spinach and the onions or shallots in quick succession. Remove and keep warm in separate dishes. Reheat the petits pois and beans if necessary.

14 To serve, wind a quarter of the Tagliatelle around the prongs of a carving fork for each serving, then place in the centre of a large, warm plate, or simply pile into a mound. Top each with a quarter of the spinach.

15 Arrange one slashed chicken breast on top of each spinach mound, so that it falls into a fan. Place the onions or shallots, petits pois and broad beans around the chicken breast.

16 Reheat the sauce and froth up with a Bamix (see page 189 for supplier) or a hand-held electric multi-blender. Ideally, spoon just the froth of the sauce over the chicken and serve the rest of the sauce separately. Garnish with the fried tarragon leaves and serve at once.

Poulet Bresse poché-grillé with sauce foie gras

Roast partridge on a bed of cabbage

GAME BIRDS AND CABBAGE WERE MADE FOR EACH OTHER. THIS PARTRIDGE DISH IS AN EASY ROAST AND, BECAUSE IT IS SERVED WITH JUST GREEN VEGETABLES, IT IS BOTH LIGHT AND FLAVOURSOME. THE BIRD IS COOKED IN TWO STAGES WITH THE BREAST AND LEGS REMOVED AFTER PAN-ROASTING TO PREVENT OVERCOOKING.

INGREDIENTS (for 2)

200ml/7fl oz/⅞ cup Brown Chicken Stock (page 18)
1 tablespoon olive oil
1 x 800g/1lb 12oz partridge, prepared for the oven
85g/3oz/¾ stick butter
1 large sprig thyme
½ small head Savoy cabbage, weighing about 250g/9oz, cut into fine julienne strips
12 baby leeks, trimmed and left whole
100g/3½oz wild mushrooms e.g. cèpes or girolles, sliced if large
sea salt and freshly ground black pepper

1 Have ready the Brown Chicken Stock and boil to reduce by half to about 100ml/3½fl oz/½ cup. Set aside.

2 Preheat the oven to 220°C/425°F/Gas Mark 7. Meanwhile, heat the oil in an ovenproof sauté pan on top of the stove and brown the bird all over, cooking and turning the bird for about 5 minutes.

3 Place the pan in the oven and roast until the partridge is only just done and the meat still pink inside – usually 7-8 minutes. Remove and allow the bird to rest, preferably covered with a butter paper or a sheet of buttered greaseproof paper. Keep the oven on.

4 Melt one-third of the butter and quickly sauté the cabbage, stirring and tossing until it starts to wilt. Pick the tips off the sprig of thyme – we call these thyme 'flowers' – and sprinkle half over the cabbage as it cooks. Season lightly and keep warm.

5 Blanch the leeks in a little boiling water, then drain well and toss in a knob of the remaining butter. Keep warm.

6 Melt half of the remaining butter and sauté the mushrooms quickly until just cooked. Season and keep warm.

7 Now, remove the breasts and legs from the carcass and return them to the pan. Discard the carcass. Cover the legs and breasts with the butter paper or buttered greaseproof paper and return to the hot oven for a further 4 minutes.

8 Reheat the stock and stir in the remaining thyme 'flowers' and the last of the butter, whisking to thicken the sauce.

9 To serve, put the cabbage in the centre of warmed plates. Cut each leg in half and place on the cabbage, then cut the breasts into 6 slices and place these on top of the legs. Garnish round the outside with the leeks and mushrooms and *nappe* (coat) with the sauce.

Roast guinea fowl with broad beans and baby asparagus

GUINEA FOWL IS A FLAVOURSOME ALTERNATIVE TO CHICKEN. WE USE BIRDS FROM FRANCE BUT A PRIME FREE-RANGE FOWL WILL BE QUITE ACCEPTABLE. THIS IS AN IDEAL DISH TO SERVE WHEN FRESH BROAD BEANS, OR FÈVES, AND YOUNG ASPARAGUS ARE IN SEASON. OUT OF SEASON, YOU CAN USE YOUNG, GOOD-QUALITY, FROZEN BROAD BEANS AND THIN ASPARAGUS.

INGREDIENTS (for 2)

400ml/14fl oz/1¾ cups Chicken Stock (page 18)
1 x guinea fowl weighing about 1.2 kg/2lb 12oz
150g/5oz fresh baby broad beans
150g/5oz young asparagus
60g/2½oz/⅔ stick butter
100g/3½oz wild mushrooms, sliced if large
1 teaspoon chopped chervil
sea salt and freshly ground black pepper

1 Have ready the Chicken Stock and set aside.

2 Remove the legs and wings from the guinea fowl and trim off the back bone. Leave the breasts intact on the carcass. Reserve the legs and wings.

3 Bring the Chicken Stock to a boil in a pan large enough to contain the fowl. Add the breasts complete with their carcass, then cover and poach for about 6-7 minutes. Remove the fowl from the stock and set aside to cool.

4 To make the sauce, add the wings and legs to the stock and boil it until reduced by half. Strain through a sieve. Discard the wings and legs and set the sauce aside.

5 Blanch the broad beans for about 2 minutes in boiling salted water. Drain, and when cool enough to handle, pop them out of their skins.

6 Blanch the asparagus for 1-2 minutes in boiling salted water, then drain and set aside.

7 Heat about one-third of the butter and sauté the mushrooms until just cooked; keep warm.

8 Preheat the oven to 220°C/425°F/Gas Mark 7. Cut the breasts from the guinea fowl carcass, and discard the bones. Heat about two-thirds of the remaining butter in an ovenproof sauté pan then cook the breasts skin-side down for 2-3 minutes or until just crisp and lightly browned.

9 Place the pan in the oven and continue to cook the breasts for about 4-5 minutes. Season, and let them rest for a few minutes before slicing each into 5-6 pieces.

10 Reheat the broad beans and asparagus in about half of the remaining butter. Place the mushrooms in the centre of each warmed dinner plate. Arrange the slices of guinea fowl on top and surround with the broad beans and asparagus.

11 Return the sauce to the boil, check the seasoning and stir in the last of the butter and the chervil. Spoon over the meat and vegetables, and serve.

Barbary duck with

Barbary duck with glazed peaches

A QUICK, SIMPLE MEAL USING BREASTS OF BARBARY DUCK, NOW READILY AVAILABLE IN LARGER SUPERMARKETS. THEY ARE SERVED WITH FRESH, CARAMELIZED PEACHES, COOKED WITH A HINT OF FIVE-SPICE POWDER.

INGREDIENTS (for 2)

400ml/14fl oz/1¾ cups Veal Stock (page 16)
1 x quantity Candied Orange Peel (page 187)
85g/3oz/¾ stick butter
6 shallots, sliced
1 teaspoon honey
1 scant teaspoon five-spice powder
1 teaspoon sherry vinegar
200ml/7fl oz/⅞ cup ruby port
100ml/3½fl oz/½ cup Madeira
2 large yellow peaches, unskinned and halved with the stones removed
1 teaspoon icing sugar
2 x 150g/5oz Barbary duck breasts
150g/5oz baby spinach leaves
sea salt and freshly ground black pepper

1 Have ready the Veal Stock and Candied Orange Peel, and set aside.

2 Heat one-third of the butter in a saucepan and sauté the shallots with the honey and about half the five-spice powder until softened and caramelized – about 7 minutes.

3 Add the vinegar and cook until evaporated. Pour in the port and Madeira and boil until the liquid is syrupy and has reduced by about two-thirds.

4 Add the Veal Stock and boil for about 15 minutes or until reduced by half, then strain through a fine sieve, rubbing gently with the back of a ladle. Season this sauce and set aside.

5 To glaze the peaches, sprinkle with the remainder of the five-spice powder and the icing sugar. Heat another third of the butter in a non-stick frying pan and gently sauté the peaches, colouring them all over. Take care not to overcook them. Set aside and reserve the pan juices in a warm place.

6 When you are ready to cook the duck breasts, preheat the oven to 220°C/425°F/Gas Mark 7. Score the fatty skin of the breasts; this ensures that the skin will become crispy when cooked.

7 Without using any oil, heat a non-stick or heavy-based frying pan until quite hot. Add the duck breasts, skin-side down, and cook for about 3 minutes, colouring all over. In this way the duck will make its own fat.

8 Cover the breasts with a butter paper or buttered greaseproof paper and cook in the oven for about 7-8 minutes, turning once or twice. Remove and allow to rest for 3 minutes before slicing each breast into 8 slices.

9 While the duck is resting, cook the spinach in a little water and the remaining butter for about one minute or until just wilted. Drain well, squeezing out lightly in a clean tea towel or kitchen paper towels.

10 Place a spinach mound in the centre of each warmed plate and arrange the sliced duck over and around each to make a pyramid shape. Cut each peach half in four and arrange on and around the duck. Trickle over the reserved pan juices. Return the sauce to the boil, check the seasoning, and spoon it over and around the meat. Garnish with Candied Orange Peel.

glazed peaches

Desserts

I truly come alive when I talk about desserts. At the Aubergine the dessert course is the one we go out of our way with to make it look breathtaking. A beautiful dessert can rival the best art. I love drawing and spend many hours with Damien, my Pastry Chef, playing around with designs. I like to think our clients are excited by desserts and see them as forbidden fruits to be savoured and enjoyed.

Ice-creams and sorbets give me pleasure too. Ours are all made in the kitchen, never bought in, and often served fresh from churning. I prefer a small scoop of heaven to a larger quantity of factory-made mediocrity.

One of my first jobs at Le Gavroche was as a night baker, starting work at midnight. This is how I learned the essential basics – brioche, sablé, sugar pastry and so on. Many chefs fear pastry but, to me, it brings great satisfaction. When I moved to Paris and the kitchens of Guy Savoy, I worked alongside the brilliant young talented Philippe Chapon and spent a great deal of time in his section, perfecting my French as well as my skills.

In the same way that a good starter sets the standard for a great meal, so a superb dessert represents the climax – it's the high spot on which our clients leave us with happy, glowing memories and intentions to return.

Tatin of pears

THE STORY OF THE TATIN SISTERS AND THEIR FAMOUS UPSIDE-DOWN APPLE TARTS IS WELL KNOWN. THE SAME IDEA WORKS EQUALLY WELL WITH PEARS. I PREFER TO COOK THE PEARS FIRST IN A CARAMEL SYRUP BEFORE BAKING THEM WITH A BUTTERY CARAMEL SAUCE AND LIGHT, HOMEMADE PUFF PASTRY. CHOOSE A FIRM FRUIT THAT HOLDS ITS SHAPE WELL, SUCH AS PACKHAMS.

INGREDIENTS (makes one 21cm/9in tart)

¼ x quantity (250g/9oz) homemade Puff Pastry (page 25)

10 firm pears e.g. Packhams

325g/11oz/1¾ cups caster sugar

50g/2oz/½ stick unsalted butter, diced

1 Have ready the homemade Puff Pastry and set aside. Peel, quarter and core the pears, then cover and set aside.

2 Put three-quarters of the sugar into a deep saucepan with about 4 table-spoons of water. Heat very slowly, stirring occasionally, until the sugar starts to dissolve. With a pot of water and a brush, wash down any sugar crystals that cling to the side of the pan; this will give you a clearer caramel.

3 When every grain of sugar has dissolved, stop stirring, raise the heat and boil the sugar until it is a rich, dark caramel. Immediately add the pear quarters, standing well back as the caramel will spit.

4 Stir the pears well to coat them. Cover with a lid, and adjust the heat to maintain a simmer for about 20 minutes, or until the pears are just softened but retain their shape and texture; during this time turn the pears once or twice. Remove from the heat. Leave the pears to cool in the caramel syrup, then chill. Drain the pears and set aside. Discard the caramel syrup.

5 Put the remaining sugar into a saucepan with 2 tablespoons of water. Dissolve the sugar and boil it to caramel stage as before. As soon as the caramel starts to smoke, whisk in the diced butter. When you have a smooth sauce, pour it into a 21cm/9in flan tin or dish which has a fixed base.

6 Roll out the pastry to a 23cm/10in diameter circle. Prick it well and transfer it to the refrigerator to rest for about 10 minutes. Preheat the oven to 200°C/400°F/Gas Mark 6.

7 Arrange the drained pears in the caramel sauce. Fit the pastry on top, tucking the edges down well to hold the pears in place. Bake for 20-25 minutes or until the pastry is golden brown and crisp. Drain the excess juices off once during baking, leaving enough juice to keep the pears moist.

8 Cool in the tin for 10 minutes then invert onto a plate and serve at room temperature.

Tatin of pears

Poached pears

Poached pears in spiced red wine

This dish is obligingly adaptable. Served on their own, poached pears make a simple, light and refreshing dessert – ideal for al fresco entertaining. At the Aubergine, we accompany them with oval scoops of My Rice Pudding (page 165), Fresh Ginger Ice-cream (page 172), a Hazelnut Tuille (page 152), a trickle of raspberry sauce and brandy snap strips. The choice of pear is important: Packhams are my favourite as they hold their shape well, but if they are unobtainable another variety of squat-shaped pear will do, as long as it is firm – almost hard. You need to start this recipe about two days in advance. The drained liquor can be re-used another time.

INGREDIENTS (for 6)

6 firm pears, ideally Packhams
1 x 75cl bottle red wine
200ml/7fl oz/⅞ cup Stock Syrup (page 23)
1 cinnamon stick
5 cardamom pods
1 star anise

1 Peel the pears thinly, leaving the stalks intact. For a decorative effect, leave some of the skin around the stalk end and, using a small, sharp knife, cut the skin into jagged points. Core the pears neatly from the base, using a small, sharp knife.

2 Place the pears in a large bowl and pour over the wine. Cover, transfer to the refrigerator and leave the pears to macerate for about one day, turning occasionally; this helps them develop a good rich colour.

3 Have ready the Stock Syrup. Drain the wine into a saucepan large enough to hold the pears upright. Add the Stock Syrup and spices, and bring to the boil. Remove from the heat and add the pears.

4 Cover with a *cartouche* – a disc of greaseproof paper cut to fit exactly inside the saucepan. Press it down on top of the pears to hold them under the liquor.

5 Adjust the heat to maintain the barest simmer and poach the pears gently for 20-30 minutes or until a skewer or knife-tip can just be pushed into the pears. Remove the pan from the heat and leave the pears to cool in the liquid. Cover and chill for one day. Drain, remove the spices and serve.

in spiced red wine

Hazelnut tuiles

WE SERVE THESE FLAT AS A BASE FOR POACHED PEARS IN SPICED RED WINE (PAGE 151), TO ACCOMPANY DAINTY SCOOPS OF ICE-CREAM, OR LIGHTLY CURLED AS PETITS FOURS.

1 Lightly whisk the egg whites to a froth then beat in the remaining ingredients. Chill for about 2 hours.

2 Preheat the oven to 180°C/350°F/Gas Mark 4. Line a baking sheet with non-stick baking parchment and spread small teaspoonfuls of the mixture over it, allowing room for some expansion and using a palette knife to scrape the tops level. For the neatest shape use a homemade template (right).

3 Bake in batches of 4-6 until light golden brown, about 7 minutes. Scoop off with a palette knife onto a wire rack where the tuiles will crisp up as they cool. For an extra flat surface to the tuiles, lay a second baking tray on top to flatten them as they cool.

4 For curved tuiles, curl them over a rolling pin while still hot. Store in an airtight container.

INGREDIENTS (for about 24)

4 egg whites
50g/2oz/¼ cup caster sugar
25g/1oz/2 tablespoons plain flour
250g/8oz/3 cups ground hazelnuts
3 scant tablespoons hazelnut oil

SHAPING TUILES

FOR PERFECT ROUND TUILES, SPREAD THE MIXTURE INTO ROUND TEMPLATES ABOUT 7.5CM/3IN DIAMETER. THESE CAN EASILY BE MADE AT HOME USING THE PLASTIC TOPS OF ICE-CREAM CONTAINERS. CUT OFF THE RAISED EDGES OF THE LID, THEN DRAW AND CUT OUT AS MANY HOLES AS WILL FIT COMFORTABLY. SPREAD A LITTLE MIXTURE INTO EACH HOLE, THEN USE A PALETTE KNIFE TO LEVEL OFF THE TOP. LIFT OFF THE TEMPLATE.

Coconut tuiles

WONDERFUL WITH NEWLY PICKED RASPBERRIES AND HOMEMADE FRESH GINGER ICE-CREAM (PAGE 172).

1 Preheat the oven to 180°C/350°F/Gas Mark 4.

2 Pass the desiccated coconut through a food processor until it is fine but not reduced to a powder.

3 Add the icing sugar and flour and process for a few more seconds until well blended, then add the egg whites and melted butter and process again until you have a smooth, slightly runny paste.

4 Line a baking sheet with non-stick baking parchment and spread small teaspoonfuls of the mixture over it, allowing room for some expansion, using a palette knife to scrape the tops level. For the neatest shape use a homemade template (above right).

5 Bake as for Hazelnut Tuiles (above) and store in an airtight container.

INGREDIENTS (for about 24)

75g/2¾oz/½ cup desiccated coconut
75g/2¾oz/½ cup icing sugar
25g/1oz/2 tablespoons plain flour
2 egg whites
50g/2oz/½ stick unsalted butter, melted and cooled

Mousse of blood-oranges

WHEN BLOOD-ORANGES ARE IN SEASON, AND THEIR FULL-FLAVOURED JUICE IS AVAILABLE, YOU HAVE THE CHANCE TO MAKE THIS REFRESHING, FEATHER-LIGHT, MOUSSE. OUT OF SEASON, USE THE FRESHLY SQUEEZED JUICE OF OTHER TYPES OF ORANGES. IN THE RESTAURANT, WE MOULD THE MOUSSES INTO PYRAMID SHAPES AND SERVE THEM WITH WAFER-THIN TRIANGLES OF DARK CHOCOLATE, BUT YOU CAN SET THE MOUSSES SIMPLY IN RAMEKINS. SERVE WITH A LIGHT-TEXTURED ORANGE AND PASSION FRUIT SAUCE.

INGREDIENTS (for 8-10)

500ml/18fl oz/2 cups fresh orange juice and 500ml/18fl oz/2 cups fresh blood-orange juice

or

1 litre/1¾ pints/4½ cups fresh orange juice

⅓ x quantity Italian Meringue (page 24)

5 leaves gelatine or 1 sachet gelatine crystals

325ml/11fl oz/1⅓ cup double cream

a little sunflower oil, to grease

FOR THE SAUCE:

500ml/18fl oz/2 cups fresh orange juice

6 passion fruits

2-3 tablespoons Stock Syrup (page 23) or 1-2 tablespoons caster sugar

1 teaspoon cornflour

1 First make the mousse: boil the 1 litre/1¾ pints/4½ cups of mixed or plain fresh orange juice until it has reduced by half to about 500ml/18fl oz/2 cups. Set aside.

2 Meanwhile, make the Italian Meringue.

3 If using leaf gelatine, soak the leaves in a bowl of iced water until softened, then remove and gently squeeze out the excess water.

4 Divide the quantity of reduced juice in half. Bring one half just to boiling point then add the soaked gelatine and stir briskly until dissolved. If using gelatine crystals, sprinkle these into the just boiled juice, whisking until dissolved. Stir in the remaining juice and strain through a fine sieve.

5 Whisk the juice very gradually into the Italian Meringue, then set aside to cool to blood temperature. Meanwhile whip the cream until it holds in soft peaks. When the orange mousse mixture has cooled, gently fold in the cream.

6 To accelerate the setting of the mousse, place the bowl in a larger bowl of iced water, stirring occasionally until the mixture is on the point of setting. Meanwhile, lightly grease 8–10 ramekin moulds.

7 Spoon the mixture into the ramekins, tapping the bases gently to ensure there are no air pockets. Chill for about 2 hours until firm.

8 While the mousses are setting, make the sauce: boil the 500ml/18fl oz/2 cups orange juice until it has reduced by half. Cut the passion fruits in half and, with a small, sharp teaspoon, scoop their pulp and seeds into the juice. Boil again for one minute. Add the Stock Syrup or sugar, tasting for sweetness and adding more if necessary. Whisk in the cornflour and cook the sauce until it has a coating consistency.

9 Remove from the heat and strain through a fine sieve. Cover with cling film to prevent a skin from forming and leave until cold. To serve, dip the ramekins briefly into boiling water, demould onto dessert plates and spoon over the sauce.

Glazed summer fruits with sauce sabayon

THIS DESSERT BRINGS TOGETHER, IN ONE MEMORABLE DISH, TWO CLASSIC SAUCES: A FRESH COULIS FRAMBOISE – WHICH CAN BE MADE WITH SLIGHTLY OVERRIPE SOFT FRUIT – AND A CHAMPAGNE SABAYON. RIPE SUMMER BERRY FRUITS ARE DRESSED LIGHTLY IN A RED COATING OF THE COULIS, THEN DRIZZLED WITH THE GOLDEN SABAYON. FOR AN ELEGANTLY SIMPLE DESSERT LEAVE IT AT THAT, BUT FOR A MORE SOPHISTICATED PRESENTATION, ARRANGE THE COULIS-COATED FRUITS AND SABAYON AROUND SCOOPS OF SORBET, WHICH MIGHT EVEN BE SERVED WITH TUILES (PAGE 152) OR IN BRANDY SNAP BASKETS.

INGREDIENTS (for 6)

about 700g/1lb 9oz selection fresh berry fruits, e.g. strawberries, raspberries, blueberries, blackberries, cherries, tayberries

FOR THE COULIS FRAMBOISE:

500g/1lb 2oz fresh or frozen raspberries (thawed if frozen)

100-125g/3½-4 oz/½-⅔ cup caster sugar

juice of ½ lemon

FOR THE SAUCE SABAYON:

3 egg yolks

50g/2oz/¼ cup caster sugar

100ml/3½ fl oz/½ cup Champagne, at room temperature

1 Pick over the fresh berry fruits, hulling or stoning where necessary. Ideally, the strawberries should be small; large ones must be at least halved.

2 To make the coulis framboise, purée the raspberries with the sugar to taste and the lemon juice, then rub through a sieve with a ladle to remove the pips. Set aside to chill, along with the berry selection, until ready to serve.

3 Make the sauce sabayon when you are ready to serve as it is best served warm. Put the egg yolks, sugar and Champagne in a heatproof bowl and set it over a saucepan of simmering water. Whisk with a hand-held electric beater or with a sturdy balloon whisk until you have a pale, creamy mixture. The foam must be sufficiently thickened so that it won't break down on cooling: you should be able to write a figure of eight with the foam when you lift the beaters. Remove and cool the foam until tepid.

4 To serve, toss the prepared fruits gently in the coulis and spoon onto serving plates. Drizzle over the sabayon sauce. If you intend serving scoops of sorbet, then place these in the centre of each plate with the fruits arranged around them in a circle.

Terrine of pink grapefruit, orange and passion fruit

SEGMENTS OF GRAPEFRUIT AND ORANGE ARE LAYERED AT RANDOM WITH BANANA AND STRAWBERRY, THEN SET IN A PASSION FRUIT JELLY FOR APPETIZING EYE-APPEAL. AN EXCELLENT PALATE CLEANSER AND LIGHT TO EAT, THIS TERRINE IS IDEAL FOR THOSE OCCASIONS WHEN A SPECIAL FRUIT DESSERT IS IN ORDER. I'VE FOUND THAT IT IS VERY POPULAR WITH CHILDREN, ESPECIALLY IF SET IN INDIVIDUAL DARIOLE MOULDS, AND IT IS PARTICULARLY REFRESHING SERVED WITH SMALL SCOOPS OF EARL GREY TEA SORBET (PAGE 173). WE OFTEN SERVE IT WITH A COULIS OF PASSION FRUIT, FINELY DICED MANGO AND STRAWBERRY.

INGREDIENTS (for 8-10)

6 pink grapefruits
8 large seedless oranges
6 passion fruits
200ml/7fl oz/⅞ cup Stock Syrup (page 23)
5 leaves gelatine or 1 sachet gelatine crystals
2 large bananas
125g/4oz fresh strawberries, hulled

1 Using a small serrated knife, cut the tops and bottoms off the citrus fruits. Cut away the remaining peel removing with it all the membrane. Holding each fruit in your hand, and working over a bowl, cut out each of the segments leaving the inner membranes behind. Discard any stray pips.

2 Place the segments on a clean tea towel to drain the juice and chill for 2 hours. Then place the segments on a fresh tea towel to drain further and chill again for another hour. This is necessary as the segments must be sufficiently dry not to leak into the jelly while setting.

3 Meanwhile, make a passion fruit syrup: halve the passion fruits and squeeze their pulp and juice into a sieve placed over a bowl. Rub the pulp and seeds through using a wooden spoon. Discard the seeds and mix the juice with the Stock Syrup.

4 If using leaf gelatine, soak the leaves in a bowl of iced water until softened, then remove and gently squeeze out the excess water.

5 Heat half of the passion fruit syrup until it boils. Remove from the heat and stir in the soaked gelatine until dissolved. If using gelatine crystals, sprinkle directly into the boiled syrup, whisking until dissolved. Mix in the remainder of the passion fruit syrup, then strain the mixture through a sieve.

6 Line a 1 kg/2lb loaf tin with cling film, leaving an overhang of about 13cm/5in all round which can later be folded over the top.

7 Mix the syrup with the citrus fruit segments then spoon about one-third into the base of the loaf tin. Peel the bananas and arrange one of them, whole, lengthways down one side of the tin; place half of the strawberries down the other side.

▶

8 Spoon over more segments and syrup. Arrange the second banana lengthways down the opposite side from the first one. Add the remaining strawberries, again on the opposite side. Finish by adding the remaining segments and juice. If you have any leftover syrup, carefully pour it in, tapping the whole tin gently and allowing the syrup to find its own level within the tin.

9 Tug the sides of the overhanging cling film gently to straighten then fold it gently over on top. Place in the refrigerator to chill overnight or until firm.

10 About 15 minutes before you are ready to unmould the terrine, transfer it to the freezer. Just before serving, unfold the cling film on top then invert the terrine onto a serving platter or board. Carefully remove all of the cling film. Cut into slices about 2cm/¾in thick, ideally with an electric carving knife, although a large serrated knife will do. Lift each slice onto a serving plate using a fish slice.

Terrine of pink grapefruit, orange and passion fruit

Apricot and

Apricot and raspberry soufflés

THERE IS NO MYSTERY TO MAKING A PERFECT HOT DESSERT SOUFFLÉ. THE TECHNIQUE IS EASY TO GRASP AND, OBLIGINGLY, IT LENDS ITSELF TO ADVANCE PREPARATION SO THAT THE SOUFFLÉ REQUIRES ONLY MINIMAL ATTENTION AND A BRIEF BAKING JUST BEFORE SERVING. A GREAT SOUFFLÉ, THOUGH, IS ONLY AS GOOD AS ITS BASE: AS LONG AS THIS IS FULL AND FLAVOURSOME, ALL THAT IS REQUIRED IS FOR THE EGG WHITES TO LIFT THE TEXTURE INTO THE SUBLIME. FOR EACH QUANTITY OF BASE MIXTURE, USE EITHER THE APRICOT OR THE RASPBERRY FRUIT PURÉE.

INGREDIENTS (makes 6 x 200ml/7fl oz or 8 x 150ml/¼ pint soufflés)

FOR THE SOUFFLÉ BASE:

⅓ x quantity Crème Pâtissière (page 22)
25g/1oz/¼ stick softened butter
50g/2oz very finely grated dark chocolate
4 egg whites
85g/3oz/⅓ cup caster sugar
a tablespoon or two of icing sugar, to dust

FOR APRICOT SOUFFLÉ:

1 x 425g/14oz can apricots in natural juice
125g/4oz/½ cup ready-to-cook dried apricots
juice of ½ lemon
1 tablespoon apricot brandy

FOR RASPBERRY SOUFFLÉ:

500g/1lb 2oz fresh or frozen raspberries, thawed if frozen
125g/4oz/½ cup caster sugar

1 Have ready the Crème Pâtissière and set aside.

2 Coat the insides of the soufflé dishes evenly with the butter. Sprinkle with the chocolate, turning the dishes and tapping out any excess. The coating helps the soufflé to rise evenly so make sure there are no gaps.

3 Make the fruit purée of your choice.

For the apricot soufflé: drain the juice from the can into a heavy pan. Add the dried apricots and just enough water to cover. Simmer until the apricots are tender and most of the liquid has reduced, about 15 minutes. Transfer to a liquidizer or food processor. Add the lemon juice, apricot brandy and the canned apricots. Blend to a smooth purée; set aside to cool.

For the raspberry soufflé: blend the fruits to a purée with the sugar then boil down to reduce by half. Cool, then rub through a sieve with a ladle to remove the pips.

4 Mix the purée of your choice with the Crème Pâtissière, blending thoroughly. The mixture can be set aside at this stage if preparing ahead.

5 Preheat the oven to 190°C/375°F/Gas Mark 5 and place the soufflé dishes on a baking sheet. Whisk the egg whites until they hold soft peaks. Gradually whisk in the sugar. Beat half the meringue mixture into the fruit pâtissière then fold in the remainder with a large metal spoon.

6 Spoon into the prepared dishes and scrape the tops level with the back of a knife. Set the ramekins on a baking sheet and bake for 10–12 minutes until the soufflés have risen dramatically and evenly.

7 Now, act fast! Have the icing sugar ready in a sieve and as you bring the soufflés out of the oven, quickly dust the tops with sugar. Set each ramekin on a plate (use a fish slice for fast action serving) and serve instantly.

raspberry soufflés

Hot chocolate fondant

An impressive finale to a meal, these small, soufflé-like fondants can be enjoyed hot, fresh from the oven. They can be frozen uncooked, then baked from frozen, so it is worth making up a batch, even if you can't eat them all at one sitting. Comforting on a cold winter's day, we serve these with a scoop of Ginger Ice-cream (page 172) garnished with Candied Orange Peel (page 187).

INGREDIENTS (for 12)

1 x quantity Italian Meringue (page 24)
150g/5oz/1¼ sticks softened unsalted butter plus 25g/1oz/¼ stick extra for greasing
350g/12oz dark chocolate at least 60% cocoa solids, broken in pieces plus 50g/2oz extra, finely grated
40g/1½ oz/¼ cup plain flour
25g/1oz/⅓ cup cocoa powder
3 teaspoons instant coffee granules
6 egg yolks

FOR THE HOT CHOCOLATE SAUCE:

150ml/¼ pint/¾ cup cold water
125g/4oz/⅔ cup sugar
40g/1½ oz/¼ cup cocoa powder
300ml/½ pint/1¼ cups double cream

1 Make up the Italian Meringue and set aside. It will hold well.

2 Melt the 25g/1oz/¼ stick of butter and use to brush the sides and bases of 12 dariole moulds or ramekin dishes, then dust with the grated chocolate, turning the moulds and tipping out excess to ensure an even coating. Set aside in the fridge to chill.

3 Place the pieces of chocolate in a heatproof bowl set over a pan of barely simmering water. Melt, stirring occasionally, then remove and cool to room temperature.

4 Sift together the flour, cocoa powder and coffee. Place the yolks and 150g/5oz/1¼ sticks softened butter in a mixing bowl and whisk together until emulsified, about 2-3 minutes.

5 Whisk the flour mixture into the yolks and butter, followed by the melted chocolate and, finally, fold in the Italian Meringue. Spoon or pipe the mixture into the prepared moulds or ramekins, tapping the moulds gently to ensure there are no air gaps, then level the tops with the back of a knife. If not immediately required, they can be placed in the freezer, otherwise wrap in cling film until ready to bake.

6 For the hot chocolate sauce, which can be prepared an hour or so before serving, put the water, sugar and cocoa powder into a saucepan and heat gently, stirring all the time, until the sugar and cocoa have dissolved. Bring to the boil, still stirring, then add the cream.

7 Return to the boil and simmer for 3-5 minutes, stirring frequently until the sauce coats the back of the spoon. Remove and cool slightly, then cover the top of the sauce loosely with cling film to prevent a skin forming.

8 When you are ready to eat the fondants, preheat the oven to 190°C/375°F/Gas Mark 5. Remove any cling film, place as many moulds or ramekins as required on a baking sheet and bake for 15 minutes, or, if they have been frozen, for about 20 minutes, until risen and firm on top.

9 Demould onto dessert plates. Pour the warm sauce over the top and serve immediately.

Hot chocolate fondant

Chocolate tart

Slim, dark and delicious – a thin, crisp pastry case contrasts sublimely with a velvety ganache of bitter chocolate that is lightly baked and set to a glossy finish. Some have said this is the best chocolate tart ever! If you wish, decorate with chocolate triangles.

INGREDIENTS (for 8-10)

⅓ x quantity Rich Sweet Pastry (page 26)
1 egg yolk beaten with a little water, to glaze
400g/14oz dark chocolate, ideally 60% cocoa solids, finely chopped
150ml/¼ pint/¾ cup milk
250ml/9fl oz/1 cup double cream
2 eggs, beaten

TO SERVE:

1 x quantity Candied Orange Peel (page 187)
whipped cream
icing sugar
cocoa powder

1 Have ready the Rich Sweet Pastry and the Candied Orange Peel.

2 On a lightly floured board, roll out the pastry dough so that it is large enough to line, with some overhang, a 21cm/9in flan tin with a removable base. Do not trim too exactly at this stage, allowing the edges to overhang slightly. Press the pastry well into the sides and make sure there are no tears. Lightly prick the base. Reserve any leftover pastry for patching.

3 Cover with foil, weigh down the base with baking beans and chill in the refrigerator for 20 minutes. Preheat the oven to 180°C/350°F/Gas Mark 4.

4 Place the flan case on a baking sheet and bake for about 10 minutes or until the pastry is just set. Remove the foil and baking beans. Using a sharp knife, trim the edges neatly. Patch any tears with leftover pastry. The aim is to have an unbroken top edge so the filling remains level.

5 Return the flan case to the oven for 5 minutes or until it just begins to colour; remove and brush with a glaze of egg yolk beaten in a little water. Lower the oven to 130°C/250°F/Gas Mark ½ and bake the case for 3 minutes to seal the glaze. Remove and set aside.

6 Meanwhile, place the chopped chocolate in a bowl. Bring the milk and cream just to the boil in a saucepan, then pour onto the chocolate, whisking until the chocolate has melted and the ingredients have amalgamated.

7 Put the beaten eggs in another bowl and pour in the chocolate mixture, whisking well. Strain through a fine sieve to ensure the mixture is smooth.

8 Return the flan case to the baking sheet and place on the oven shelf which you have lifted out slightly. Pour the chocolate mixture into the case, taking the mixture as high up the sides as you dare. It should be almost flush with the top.

9 Carefully reposition the shelf and bake the tart for about 25 minutes or until the filling has started to set. Turn off the oven, leaving the tart inside for a further 30 minutes, then remove and set aside to cool completely. When cool, push up the base to remove from the tin. Garnish with whipped cream and Candied Orange Peel dusted with icing sugar and cocoa powder.

Chocolate tart

Pavé au chocolat

THE ULTIMATE CHOCOLATE MOUSSE TO SERVE WITH RASPBERRIES OR WITH A VANILLA ICE-CREAM, OR WITH BOTH. IN THE AUBERGINE, WE SERVE THIS MOUSSE OF DARK CHOCOLATE ON A CRISP BASE OF WHITE CHOCOLATE IN SMALL INDIVIDUAL MOULDS. AT HOME YOU MAY FIND IT EASIER TO MAKE ONE LARGE MOUSSE. ANOTHER OPTION WOULD BE TO SKIP THE BASE AND JUST SPOON THE MOUSSE ONLY INTO ELEGANT WINE GLASSES. I HAVE ADAPTED THE BASE FOR DOMESTIC COOKS SINCE IN THE RESTAURANT WE USE SPECIAL INGREDIENTS IMPORTED FROM FRANCE: CRUSHED WAFERS KNOWN AS *PAILLETTE FEUILLETINE* AND A PRALINE PASTE. FOR A GOOD, STRONG CHOCOLATE FLAVOUR, CHOOSE CHOCOLATE WITH ABOUT 60% COCOA SOLIDS. THIS DESSERT CAN BE MADE AND FROZEN AHEAD.

INGREDIENTS (for 8-10)

FOR THE WHITE CHOCOLATE BASE:

85g/3oz white chocolate, broken into pieces
2 tablespoons double cream
1 teaspoon liquid glucose
3 Pompadour ice-cream fan wafers or 85g/3oz/3 cups cornflakes, crushed into fine crumbs

FOR THE DARK CHOCOLATE MOUSSE:

300g/10oz dark chocolate, broken in pieces
4 egg yolks
125g/4oz/1⁄3 cup caster sugar
90ml/3fl oz/1⁄3 cup cold water
300ml/½ pint/1¼ cups double cream
100ml/3½fl oz/½ cup milk

TO SERVE:

fresh raspberries
vanilla ice-cream

1 For the base, melt the white chocolate with the cream, in a bowl set over a pan of gently simmering water, stirring occasionally until smooth. Remove the bowl and set aside. When cool, beat in the liquid glucose.

2 Stir the crushed fan wafers or cornflakes into the chocolate. Place the outside ring of a 21cm/9in cake tin, without the base, onto a flat serving plate and press the mixture into it with the back of a spoon. It should be nice and even. Transfer to the refrigerator.

3 For the mousse, melt the dark chocolate in a bowl set over a pan of gently simmering water, stirring occasionally. Take care not to let it over-heat or it will 'seize' and become difficult to stir to a smooth cream. Remove the bowl from the pan and cool to room temperature.

4 Put the egg yolks, sugar and water into a larger bowl. Set it over a pan of simmering water. Using a balloon whisk or a hand-held electric beater, whisk until you have a thick, pale gold foam. You should be able to draw a figure of eight with the trail of foam when it is the right consistency. Fold in the melted chocolate with a metal spoon then chill in the refrigerator.

5 When the chocolate mixture is cool, whip the cream and milk together in another bowl until soft peaks form. Fold half of this cream mixture into the chocolate mixture and, once it is incorporated, fold in the remainder. This two-stage process will ensure a nice light texture. Spoon the mousse mixture onto the crushed wafer base in the cake tin, spreading evenly to ensure a level surface. Return to the refrigerator to set.

6 When the mousse is firm, run the tip of a knife around the ring and lift it away. Slide a palette knife under the base of the flan to loosen it, but keep it on the same plate. Serve with raspberries and vanilla ice-cream.

My rice pudding

A well-loved favourite to which I add a sophisticated touch of crème anglaise. The creamy, mousse-like texture of this rice pudding means it has great appeal as a cold dessert, and it can be moulded into little ovals and served as an accompaniment to fruit such as Poached Pears in Spiced Red Wine (page 151). However, it is equally acceptable when presented as a dessert in its own right, served in small custard cups or elegant stemmed glasses and, perhaps, trickled with a purée of mango or prunes. Good, too, served hot as a traditional rice pudding.

INGREDIENTS (for 8-10)

500ml/18fl oz/2 cups milk
500ml/18fl oz/2 cups double cream
1 vanilla pod
180g/6oz/1 cup round-grain pudding rice
12 egg yolks
180g/6oz/⅞ cup caster sugar

1 In a large heavy-based saucepan, bring the milk and cream to scalding point. Meanwhile, split the vanilla pod, scrape out the seeds and add these, along with the pod itself, to the saucepan.

2 Stir in the rice and bring to the boil. Lower to a slow simmer and continue cooking, stirring occasionally, for 15-20 minutes, or until the rice is soft and the mixture reduced and thickened.

3 In a large bowl beat the yolks with the sugar until the mixture is pale and smooth. When the rice mixture is ready, beat it gradually into the egg mixture.

4 Return the mixture to the pan and very gently reheat until it thickens again, stirring occasionally. Cool, stirring once or twice to stop a skin forming, then chill over a bowl of iced water until set.

5 To serve as an accompaniment, shape into quenelles (page 173) using 2 dessertspoons. Alternatively, press into small moulds using round cutters placed on dessert plates.

Cassonades

AT THE AUBERGINE, WE SERVE THESE CASSONADES, OR CUSTARDS, IN A VARIETY OF FLAVOURS IN DAINTY CUSTARD CUPS, ARRANGING A SELECTION OF THREE AS AN INDIVIDUAL SERVING. BUT THEY ARE EQUALLY GOOD SERVED SINGLY MADE IN A LARGER CUSTARD CUP OR RAMEKIN. POPULAR FLAVOURS INCLUDE VANILLA, SARRIETTE (DRIED WILD THYME) AND COFFEE – THE LATTER EMPLOYING A HOMEMADE ESSENCE (BELOW). BUT WHY, YOU MAY ASK, DO WE USE UHT MILK? THE ANSWER IS IT HELPS TO STABILIZE THE CUSTARD MIXTURE DURING BAKING AND IT ALSO MEANS THAT WE CAN USE FEWER EGGS.

INGREDIENTS (for 6)

FOR THE BASIC CUSTARD:

500ml/18fl oz/2 cups double cream
100ml/3½fl oz/½ cup UHT full cream milk
4 egg yolks
85g/3oz/⅓ cup caster sugar
demerara sugar, for sprinkling

FOR THE FLAVOUR VARIATIONS:

2 vanilla pods, split and seeds scraped out
or
25g/1oz sarriette sprigs (dried wild thyme)
or
2 sprigs fresh thyme
or
125g/4oz/½ cup coffee beans plus 1 tablespoon Homemade Coffee Essence (below)

1 Put the cream, milk and the flavouring of your choice into a large saucepan and bring it to scalding point. Preheat the oven to 120°C/225°F/Gas Mark Low.

2 Meanwhile whisk the egg yolks in a large bowl. When the milk just starts to rise up the sides of the pan, pour it onto the yolks, whisking continuously, then whisk in the sugar until dissolved.

3 Strain through a fine sieve, discard the flavourings, then pour into 6 ramekin dishes which have been set out on a baking sheet. Bake for 35-45 minutes until just set, then cool and chill until firm.

4 To serve, sprinkle with a light, even layer of demerara sugar and place under a very hot, preheated grill to glaze; or, if you have one, use a hand-held flame torch to caramelize the sugar. Cool and serve.

Homemade coffee essence

INGREDIENTS (makes about 350ml/12fl oz/1½ cups)

300g/10oz/1½ cups caster sugar
drop of liquid glucose
about 4 tablespoons cold water
100g/3½oz/2 cups instant coffee granules

1 In a heavy-based saucepan, moisten the caster sugar with a small drop of liquid glucose and the water. Dissolve slowly, over a low to medium heat, stirring occasionally, brushing the pan sides down with water if crystals start to appear.

2 When every grain has dissolved, stop stirring, raise the heat and boil the syrup steadily until it just begins to caramelize. Remove from the heat and carefully mix in the instant coffee granules.

3 Cool, then bottle and use as required.

Cassonades

Crème brûlée with roasted rhubarb

HERE, RHUBARB AND CUSTARD IS GIVEN A SOPHISTICATED TREATMENT. THE BRÛLÉE CUSTARD IS MADE DIFFERENTLY FROM REGULAR CUSTARD: SUGAR IS ADDED AFTER THE MILK HAS BEEN BEATEN ONTO THE YOLKS, RESULTING IN A THICK MIXTURE THAT ALLOWS THE VANILLA SEEDS TO BE HELD IN SUSPENSION. WE SERVE THIS WITH A TINY SCOOP OF RASPBERRY SORBET AND A MINT SPRIG.

INGREDIENTS (for 6)

250g/9oz rhubarb, leaves discarded
15g/½oz/1 tablespoon unsalted butter
1 dessertspoon clear honey
2 vanilla pods
350ml/12fl oz/1½ cups double cream
125ml/4fl oz/½ cup UHT whole milk
6 egg yolks
75g/2½oz/⅓ cup caster sugar

TO SERVE:

Dried Strawberries (page 187) (optional)
Jus de Fraises (page 22)
demerara sugar, for sprinkling

1 Have ready the Dried Strawberries if using, and the Jus de Fraises.

2 Peel away the stringy, coarse ribs of the rhubarb then cut the stalks first into 4cm/1½in lengths, then into bâtons. Heat the butter and honey in a large frying pan until bubbling, then add the rhubarb in a single layer and 'roast' gently for about 5 minutes, turning carefully, until softened but still whole.

3 Drain in a sieve then spread out on a clean tea towel to absorb excess moisture. Change the towel twice more. It is important to drain the rhubarb thoroughly so that it doesn't rise during baking.

4 Meanwhile, line the base of six ramekin dishes with discs of greaseproof paper. When the rhubarb is quite dry, divide between the dishes, spreading the pieces neatly over the bases. Arrange the ramekins on a baking sheet.

5 Slit the vanilla pods, scrape out the seeds and mix with the cream. Put the cream, milk and empty pods into a large saucepan and bring slowly to the boil.

6 Meanwhile, in a large bowl, beat the yolks with a whisk until smooth and a paler shade of yellow. Preheat the oven to 120°C/225°F/Gas Mark Low.

7 When the cream mixture starts to boil and rise, pour it, in stages, onto the yolks, whisking continuously. Stir in the caster sugar until it has all dissolved. Strain through a fine sieve into a jug and discard the vanilla pods.

8 Pour a little of the custard over the rhubarb in the ramekins and transfer to the oven for 20 minutes or until the mixture has set enough to hold the rhubarb in place. Pour in the remaining custard and cook for a further 45-60 minutes or until lightly set. The custard is ready when, if tipped, it comes away slowly from the sides of the mould and is slightly wobbly in the centre,

9 Cool, then chill until quite firm. To unmould, run a table knife round the edge of each ramekin and invert onto a plate. Remove the paper discs.

10 Sprinkle the custards with demerara sugar, then caramelize, either with a hand-held blowtorch, or by placing under a hot grill. Tuck the Dried Strawberries just beneath the top of each brûlée and spoon round the Jus de Fraises.

Crème brûlée with

roasted rhubarb

Ice-creams and sorbets

For me, there is little to match the satisfaction of making homemade ice-creams. What particularly appeals is the sheer variety of flavours one can create, reflecting an originality and subtlety that becomes truly unique. There is a good practical reason, too, for making ice-cream at home – it is very simple and invariably popular!

At the Aubergine, we use ice-creams and sorbets to accompany many of our desserts, spooning the frozen mixtures into quenelle shapes using teaspoons, or serving as moulds. But they are also impressive enough to stand alone: a selection of, say, three or four can be made ahead and stored ready for spontaneous serving. If frozen ahead in this way, the ices will require a resting period of around 10 minutes at room temperature to soften their texture sufficiently for scooping and serving.

Ice-creams and sorbets consist of flavourings added to the basic mixtures: Crème Anglaise for ice-creams, and syrups for sorbets. Intense cold can mask flavours and this must be compensated for by preparing mixtures that are well sweetened and well flavoured.

Crème anglaise

My ice-creams are made by adding flavourings to a rich base of Crème Anglaise. The flavourings are added either at the beginning of making the custard, for example with vanilla, cinnamon or ginger ice-creams, or at the end as with prune and Armagnac ice-cream. Ice-creams are best churned during freezing in electric machines which break down ice crystals effortlessly into a silky texture. In the absence of an electric ice-cream maker, most mixtures must be beaten by hand with a strong balloon whisk three or four times during freezing to break up the ice crystals and loosen the texture although the result will not be as smooth as machine-churned ices.

INGREDIENTS (for 6 generous servings or 8-10 smaller ones)

500ml/18fl oz/2 cups milk
500ml/18fl oz/2 cups double cream
12 egg yolks
180g/6oz/⅞ cup caster sugar

1 In a large heavy-based saucepan, heat the milk, cream and any flavouring, stirring occasionally, until the mixture comes just up to the boil. Remove from the heat and allow the flavourings to infuse for 10 minutes.
2 Meanwhile, set a large mixing bowl on a damp cloth – to steady the bowl – and whisk together the yolks and sugar until the mixture turns pale golden and you can draw a figure of eight across the surface.
3 Return the flavoured milk and cream to the heat and bring back to the boil. When the mixture begins to creep up the sides of the pan, immediately remove from the heat and pour half of it into the yolks and sugar, whisking well. When the mixture is well blended, reheat the remaining creamy milk and whisk this in too until well blended.
4 Pour the custard mixture back into the pan and, on the lowest possible heat, stir for approximately 2 minutes using a wooden spoon, until the mixture coats the back of the spoon and has a consistency similar to that of double cream. Your finger should be able to draw a line through the mixture on the back of the spoon that will make a definite parting. Do not allow the custard to boil or it will curdle. If you have a sugar thermometer, you can check this by aiming for a reading of 82°C/175°F.
5 Strain the mixture into another bowl through a fine sieve, discarding any flavourings, and cool down as quickly as possible by standing in a larger bowl of iced water. Stir occasionally to prevent a skin forming. Cool then chill until ready to freeze.

FLAVOUR VARIATIONS:

Enough for one quantity of Crème Anglaise:

Vanilla Ice-cream: *scrape the seeds from 2 split pods into the milk and cream, and add the empty pods too.*

Cinnamon Ice-cream: *add 1 stick of cinnamon and 2½ level teaspoons ground cinnamon to the milk and cream.*

Fresh Ginger Ice-cream: *add 60g/2¼oz peeled and chopped fresh root ginger into the milk and cream.*

Prune and Armagnac Ice-cream: *pit and finely chop 150g/5oz plump French prunes. Macerate in 3 tablespoons of Armagnac for at least 8 hours or overnight. Make the ice-cream up to the churning stage and when about three-quarters of the way through churning (the end of step 7), stir in the fruit and liqueur.*

CHURNING AND FREEZING:

6 If you are using an ice-cream maker follow the manufacturer's instructions to churn the Crème Anglaise. If you don't have a machine, beat the mixture by hand using a balloon whisk or a strong fork. Pour the chilled mixture into a shallow container and set in the coldest part of the freezer, or switch on the fast-freeze switch, depending on your type of freezer.

7 As ice crystals begin to form around the edges, remove the container from the freezer and use a strong balloon whisk or a large fork to beat the crystals into the rest of the mixture. Return to the freezer. Repeat this process about 3-4 times. The ice-cream will gradually become stiffer, yet softer in texture.

8 When the ice-cream is of a firm dropping consistency, cover and leave in the freezer until it is required. If you have made the ice-cream ahead of time and it is very firm, allow it to soften for about 10 minutes at room temperature.

SHAPING QUENELLES

TO SERVE THE ICE-CREAM AS QUENELLES, SCOOP THE SLIGHTLY SOFTENED ICE-CREAM AND SHAPE BETWEEN 2 TEASPOONS, THEN PLACE ON A TRAY. RETURN TO THE FREEZER TO FIRM. THEY ARE THEN READY FOR PLACING ON PLATES WHEN YOU ARE ABOUT TO SERVE.

Sorbets

THE BASIC METHOD FOR SORBETS IS SIMPLE: SUGAR IS DISSOLVED IN WATER OR JUICE THEN BOILED GENTLY, CHILLED AND CHURNED. PARADOXICALLY, ACID, IN THE FORM OF LEMON OR LIME JUICE, HELPS INTENSIFY THE SWEETNESS

Earl Grey tea sorbet

1 In a large, heavy-based saucepan, bring the water and sugar slowly to the boil, stirring gently with a wooden spoon, until the sugar has completely dissolved. Raise the heat and let the syrup boil rapidly for 5 minutes.

2 Remove from the heat, add the Earl Grey tea bags and leave them to infuse for 10 minutes. Add the lime and lemon juices then strain the liquid into a jug. Cool and chill.

3 Churn in an ice-cream machine to a soft ice texture and either serve straight away or transfer to a freezer container and store in the freezer for up to two weeks. Allow to soften slightly at room temperature before serving or shape into quenelles (above).

INGREDIENTS (for 6 generous servings or 8-10 smaller ones)

900ml / 1½ pints / 4 cups cold water

250g / 9oz / 1¼ cups caster sugar

6 Earl Grey teabags

juice of 1 lime

juice of 1 lemon

Blood-orange sorbet

INGREDIENTS (for 10 generous servings or 15 smaller ones)

500ml/18fl oz/2 cups cold water
400g/14oz/2 cups caster sugar
900ml/1½ pints/4 cups fresh blood-orange juice
juice of 1 lemon

1 In a large, heavy-based saucepan, bring the water and sugar slowly to the boil, stirring gently with a wooden spoon, until the sugar has completely dissolved. Raise the heat and let the syrup boil rapidly for 5 minutes.

2 Remove from the heat, add the orange and lemon juices, then strain. Cool and chill.

3 Churn in an ice-cream machine to a soft ice texture and either serve straight away or transfer to a freezer container and store in the freezer for up to two weeks. Allow to soften slightly at room temperature before serving or shape into quenelles (page 173).

Pineapple sorbet

INGREDIENTS (for 6 generous servings or 8-10 smaller ones)

1 ripe medium pineapple
600ml/1 pint/2½ cups cold water
250g/9oz/1½ cups caster sugar

1 Peel, core and chop the pineapple into small chunks.

2 In a large, heavy-based saucepan, bring the water and sugar slowly to the boil, stirring gently with a wooden spoon, until the sugar has completely dissolved. Raise the heat and let the syrup boil rapidly for 5 minutes.

3 Stir in the pineapple and poach until soft, about 10 minutes. Cool slightly, then purée and strain. Cool completely and chill.

4 Churn in an ice-cream machine to a soft ice texture and either serve straight away or transfer to a freezer container and store in the freezer for up to two weeks. Allow to soften slightly at room temperature before serving or shape into quenelles (page 173).

Bitter chocolate sorbet

THIS TAKES CHOCOLATE ICE-CREAM INTO A NEW DIMENSION – DARK AND DELICIOUS WITHOUT BEING RICH AND CREAMY. ALTHOUGH SIMPLE TO MAKE, THIS ICE CAN ONLY BE MADE USING AN ELECTRIC ICE-CREAM MAKER WITH ITS OWN BUILT-IN FREEZER UNIT.

INGREDIENTS (for 6 generous servings or 8-10 smaller ones)

250ml/9fl oz/1 cup milk
250ml/9fl oz/1 cup cold water
150g/5oz/¾ cup caster sugar
50g/2oz/2 tablespoons liquid glucose
200g/7oz dark chocolate, at least 60% cocoa solids, broken into pieces

1 Put the milk, water, sugar and glucose on to the heat, stirring until dissolved, then bring to the boil.

2 Remove from the heat and add the chocolate, stirring until smooth.

3 Return to the heat, bring back to the boil, then strain through a fine sieve and leave to cool until warm and still runny.

4 Pour into an electric ice-cream machine and churn until smooth and a soft frozen texture. Cover and store until required. This can be shaped into quenelles for serving (page 173).

Sorbets

Parfaits

My parfaits are a combination of a mousse-like Pâte à Bombe, meringue mixture and a flavoured whipped cream. Parfaits do not need to be churned during freezing. This is because the high percentage of meringue means that air has already been incorporated which makes the texture smoother. This makes them easier to mould, either in individual ramekins, or in a loaf tin when it can be served cut in slices. Alternatively, a frozen parfait mixture can be shaped into quenelles using 2 dessertspoons (page 173).

Banana parfait

In the restaurant I serve this with caramel and cocoa-bean wafers and slices of banana dipped in hot caramel. For a simpler presentation it works well served with Bitter Chocolate Sorbet (page 174) as here, Dried Strawberries (page 187), with the glazed fruits from the Glazed Summer Fruits with Sauce Sabayon recipe (page 154) or with slices of the Tatin of Pears (page 148). Use very ripe bananas for the best flavour.

INGREDIENTS (for 10-12 servings)

1 x quantity Pâte à Bombe (page 23)
½ x quantity French Meringue (page 24)
300ml/½ pint/1¼ cups double cream
3 very ripe bananas, mashed to a thick purée
2 tablespoons Crème de Banane or white rum
1 x quantity Bitter Chocolate Sorbet (page 174)
few sprigs mint

1 Whisk together the Pâte à Bombe and the French Meringue mixtures. They should be in roughly equal amounts by volume.

2 Lightly whip the cream to the same consistency as the Pâte à Bombe and French Meringue mixture then whisk both mixtures together.

3 Finally, whisk in the banana purée and liqueur. Pour or pipe into ramekins, a long loaf tin or a large freezer container. Freeze until firm.

4 About 30 minutes before serving, transfer the parfait from the freezer to the refrigerator.

5 To unmould the parfait just before serving, run the tip of a knife around the edge of the mould to loosen it. Wrap the mould for several minutes in a towel wrung out in very hot water, then invert the mould onto a serving plate.

6 Serve each slice with a scoop of Bitter Chocolate Sorbet and garnish with the mint sprigs.

Banana parfait

Finishing touches

This is where we can show off without overt boasting. These subtle touches, which show loving care, are all prepared ahead when we have time, then stored in airtight tins ready in seconds for setting off our chosen dish: whether Shredded Leeks to garnish Roasted Monkfish with Red Wine Sauce (page 113) or Dried Strawberries to decorate Crème Brûlèe with Roasted Rhubarb (page 168) or, perhaps, a mousse or an ice-cream.

The technique of drying slices of fruit, for use as a finishing touch, provides great scope. I do enjoy the process as the end results make stunning decorations, adding a breathtaking finishing touch to simple desserts. There are a great many fruits that you can use, including apples, strawberries, mangoes and pineapples, but the basic principles are always the same.

Shredded leeks

ONE OF OUR LIGHT GARNISHES WHICH IS EASY TO MAKE IN QUANTITY AND STORE IN AN AIRTIGHT POLYTHENE CONTAINER. INSTRUCTIONS ARE GIVEN FOR ONE LEEK (WHICH MAKES A LOT) BUT YOU MAY WISH TO INCREASE THE AMOUNT.

INGREDIENTS

1 large leek

vegetable oil, for frying

1 Trim the leek of roots and tops, then slit down to the centre without cutting in half. Remove the inner section of the leek (use this in another dish) leaving about 3-4 outer layers.

2 Cut the leek layers into 10cm/4in lengths and fold each section in two horizontally, i.e. the opposite way to its natural fold. Using a very sharp cook's knife, shred finely. Repeat with the remainder of the leek.

3 Line a baking sheet with greaseproof paper and scatter the shreds loosely over. Bake in the oven set at its lowest heat, about 120°C/225°F/Gas Mark Low. If it is still too hot, prop the oven door ajar. Cook for about 2 hours or until the leek shreds feel dry and crisp, yet still retain a green colour.

4 To serve, deep fry in hot oil, heated to about 170°C/325°F, for just a few seconds to crisp and colour them even further. Drain and serve in delicate mounds as a garnish.

Candied aubergine slices

THESE LIGHTLY CARAMELIZED SLICES ARE DELICIOUS SERVED AS A GARNISH TO SAVOURY DISHES SUCH AS THE SALAD OF ROASTED LANGOUSTINE (PAGE 54) AND RUMP OF LAMB NIÇOISE (PAGE 135).

INGREDIENTS (makes 16 slices)

1 small long thin aubergine, ideally about 5cm/2in in diameter

sea salt, to dégorge

caster sugar, to dégorge

olive oil, for frying

1 Cut 16 thin slices from the aubergine. Layer the slices in a colander, sprinkling each layer lightly and evenly with sea salt and caster sugar in equal proportions. Leave to dégorge for 15 minutes so that any bitter juices are drawn out, leaving the slices limp.

2 Pat the slices dry in a clean tea towel. In a large frying pan add enough olive oil to give a depth of 1cm/½in. Heat the oil to about 170°C/325°F and fry the slices until crisp but not too brown. Drain on kitchen paper towels.

Shredded leeks

Apple castles

Drying fruits

IDEALLY, THE OVEN MUST BE SET AT AROUND 80°C/170°F. THIS SETTING IS OFTEN LOWER THAN MANY DOMESTIC OVENS CAN MANAGE, UNLESS THE MODEL IS AN OLD-FASHIONED ONE FEATURING A PERMANENT PILOT LIGHT, OR A VERY MODERN ONE WITH A DEFROST SETTING. IF YOUR OVEN CANNOT OBLIGE, TURN IT TO ITS LOWEST SETTING, USUALLY 110°C/225°F, AND PROP THE DOOR AJAR. YOU MAY FIND IT HELPFUL TO HAVE AN OVEN THERMOMETER IN THE OVEN TO CHECK THE TEMPERATURE. ALTHOUGH APPLES TAKE ONLY AROUND 2-3 HOURS TO DRY, SOME FRUITS, SUCH AS STRAWBERRIES, CAN TAKE UP TO 18 HOURS, SO BE PATIENT. THE FRUIT MUST BE SLICED THINLY AND THE SLICES ARRANGED WITHOUT TOUCHING EACH OTHER ON BAKING SHEETS LINED WITH NON-STICK SILICONE BAKING SHEETING SUCH AS BAKE-O-GLIDE (SEE PAGE 189 FOR STOCKISTS). UNFORTUNATELY, REGULAR BAKING PARCHMENT IS UNSUITABLE FOR THIS TECHNIQUE AS IT CAN GET WET CAUSING THE FRUIT TO STICK. ALL THESE DRIED FRUITS CAN BE MADE AHEAD OF TIME IN LARGE BATCHES AND STORED IN WELL-SEALED, AIRTIGHT CONTAINERS.

Apple castles

IN A PROFESSIONAL KITCHEN, WE FIND A USE FOR EVERYTHING – EVEN APPLE SKINS! THIS MAY TAKE YOU BACK TO YOUR CHILDHOOD WHEN YOU TRIED TO PEEL AN APPLE IN ONE GO, WITH THE SKIN SWIRLING INTO A CONTINUOUS SPIRAL, EXCEPT THAT WE THEN DRY OUT THE SPIRAL AND CURL IT INTO AN ARTISTIC SCULPTURE.

INGREDIENTS

3–4 Granny Smith apples
150ml/¼ pint/¾ cup Stock Syrup (page 23)
juice of ½ lemon

1 Peel the apples thinly in a quite narrow continuous spiral without breaking. Dip into a bowl filled with the Stock Syrup mixed with the lemon juice and place, skin-side up and in a flat curly 'S' shape, on a baking sheet lined with non-stick silicone baking sheeting. Set the oven to its lowest possible setting (see above) and leave the skins to dry for about 2½ hours.
2 To shape, kneel by the oven with a cooking rack in front of you. Pick up a length of dried skin and curl it into a 3-D shape, like a sculpture. This will start to harden and crisp so you need to work quite fast. The curling process may take a little time to perfect, so persevere. Store in a large airtight container.

Apple tuiles

WE SERVE THESE AS A DECORATION FOR DESSERTS AND AS AN ACCOMPANIMENT TO SORBETS AND ICE-CREAMS, BUT THEY ALSO MAKE A LOVELY SWEET SNACK, RESEMBLING AS THEY DO APPLE CRISPS. JUST TWO APPLES WILL MAKE A LOT OF SLICES. IT HELPS TO HAVE A MANDOLIN TO DO THE SLICING.

INGREDIENTS

2 Granny Smith apples
150ml/¼ pint/¾ cup Stock Syrup (page 23)
juice of ½ lemon, strained

1 Neatly core the apples, making sure the coring is quite central. Pour the Stock Syrup into a bowl and mix with the lemon juice.

2 Using a mandolin or a very sharp knife, cut the apples into slices about 1mm/$\frac{1}{16}$in thick.

3 Drop these into the lemon syrup to just coat, then arrange in a single layer on a baking sheet lined with non-stick silicone baking sheeting.

4 Dry out in the oven on its lowest possible setting (see page 183) for about 2 hours, then remove the slices in relays and place them over a rolling pin to curl. If you remove them all at once they will crisp before you can curl them. Alternatively, if you have a French baguette tin, curl the slices inside the tubes. However, if you find curling difficult, bear in mind the slices also look attractive served flat.

Apple tuiles

Dried strawberries

IF OTHER FRUITS CAN BE DRIED, WHY NOT STRAWBERRIES? AFTER SOME HOURS OF EXPERIMENTING, I CAME UP WITH A WAY OF PRESERVING ONE OF THE BEST-LOVED SUMMER FRUITS. THEIR WAFER-THIN ELEGANCE MAKES THEM IDEAL AS DELICATE DECORATIONS FOR BRÛLÉES AND ICE-CREAMS.

INGREDIENTS

Large well-shaped strawberries, hulled

1 Thinly slice the strawberries lengthways. Discard the end slices and lay the large, middle slices out on baking sheets lined with non-stick silicone baking sheeting. Make sure the slices don't touch each other.

2 Dry out in the oven on its lowest possible setting (see page 183) for 14-18 hours until crisp and dry. Test one by snapping it in half. The colour will have become more muted but the beautiful translucence more than makes up for it.

Candied orange peel

THIS MAKES A VERY VERSATILE GARNISH FOR BOTH SWEET AND SAVOURY DISHES AND IS AN EXCELLENT USE FOR LEFTOVER ORANGE PEEL.

INGREDIENTS

2-3 oranges

150ml/¼ pint/¾ cup Stock Syrup (page 23)

1 Peel the oranges thinly, making sure there is no bitter pith attached to the skin, and cut the peel into very fine julienne strips

2 Blanch the peel in boiling water for 1 minute, drain then refresh in cold water. Pat dry with kitchen paper towels.

3 Pour the Stock Syrup into a saucepan and bring to the boil. Add the blanched peel and simmer for about 10 minutes.

4 Using a slotted spoon, remove the peel from the Stock Syrup and spread the strips out on a tray lined with non-stick silicone baking sheeting. Place the tray in a very low oven, or a warm airing cupboard, for about 45-50 minutes to dry out.

Dried strawberries

Glossary

Aigre-doux A sauce combining sweet and sour flavourings.

Amuse-gueule Literally, a mouth amusement, a bite-sized canapé served at the very start of a meal to tease the palate.

Bamix A hand-held electric blender used to purée or beat foods until smooth, or to whisk up liquids into a cappuccino froth. (For supplier see page 189.)

Beignet A sweet or savoury deep-fried fritter.

Blanch To dip fresh food briefly into boiling water to soften it on the outside whilst the centre remains crisp. Blanched food is often then 'refreshed' in cold water (see right).

Brandade A dish of flaked fish mixed with other ingredients, usually including potatoes.

Caramelize To heat or cook a food until it starts to turn a luscious golden brown and takes on a slightly smoky flavour.

Cassonade A custard with a burnt sugar topping. From the French word *cassant*, meaning brittle.

Caul fat The thin membrane lining of a pig's stomach used in charcuterie and sausage-making. Used as a wrapping, it bathes ingredients in moisture, holds them together and leaves a delicate lacy pattern when cooked. Caul fat can be ordered in advance from speciality butchers and must be soaked before use.

Clarify To remove the solid deposits from liquids by straining through a cloth, e.g. melted butter.

Concasse Evenly chopped food such as Tomato Concasse (page 97).

Confit Literally, a conserve. The food is cooked very gently in fat or oil and then stored in the same fat or oil.

Court-bouillon A flavoured or aromatic liquid in which to poach fish, seafood or vegetables.

Crépinette A minced patty of meat encased in caul fat and fried.

Dariole Originally a small cake, now more often a term used to describe small individual moulds with sloping sides.

Deglaze To dilute pan juices produced when frying meats and vegetables, using water, stock, vinegar or wine.

Dégorge To encourage the release of bitter juices from ingredients such as aubergines, cucumbers, courgettes and tomatoes by sprinkling them with salt and sugar. This process also softens them sufficiently for gentle frying.

Infuse To steep herbs, spices or other flavourings in a hot liquid so that they impart their delicate fragrance.

Julienne Food, generally vegetables, cut into very thin strips. Named in honour of an 18th-century Paris chef, Jean Julien.

Liaison Combining thickening agents with a liquid, e.g. eggs and cream, flour and milk.

Mille-feuille Literally, 1,000 leaves, normally associated with high-rise puff pastry desserts but now often used to describe finely layered foods.

Muslin Very fine, loosely woven cotton cloth used for wrapping foods or to line colanders and sieves for filtering liquids until very clear. It can be ordered through kitchen mail-order companies. Well worn, but clean, tea towels or disposable kitchen cloths make suitable alternatives.

Nage From the French verb *nager*, to swim. A light clear 'broth' or court-bouillon made with fish or vegetables. At the Aubergine, we make Vegetable Nage each day and use it in conjunction with meat and fish stocks to lighten them without diluting the flavour. It is also a good all-purpose stock and very simple to make.

Nappe To coat food thinly and evenly with a sauce using a tablespoon. The correct technique is important! The sauce should flow from the side of the spoon, not the tip, so that it glides evenly over the food.

Pavé Literally, a slab, this is used to describe food cut into a neat shape, usually a square or rectangle, e.g. fish or chocolate cake.

Non-stick baking parchment Oven-proof silicone-coated material used to prevent food and mixtures from sticking during baking. Sold under several brand names including Bake-O-Glide. Re-usable and durable, and great for home-dried fruits, as well as meringues and tuiles.

Reduce To boil a liquid in an uncovered pan. As the liquid evaporates, the flavour becomes more concentrated.

Refresh To plunge just boiled vegetables into ice-cold water for about 1-2 minutes to stop cooking and preserve the colour, flavour and texture. After draining, the vegetables are kept chilled and covered ready for reheating and serving.

Roast To cook food exposed to open fire or in the oven. In restaurant kitchens the term is also used to describe cooking in a hot, lightly-oiled frying pan, starting on top of the stove, then sometimes finishing in a hot oven.

Quenelle Food shaped into an oval using 2 spoons. We shape ice-cream, whipped cream and even rice pudding into decorative quenelles to make an excellent garnish.

Sauté To fry food quickly in a small amount of hot oil. From the French word *sauter*, to jump, which the food appears to do when the frying pan is shaken.

Sweat To fry food, generally vegetables, very gently in a covered pan, using only a small amount of oil so that beads of steam fall back onto the food to baste and moisten it during the cooking process.

Tian A mould of finely chopped fresh vegetables.

Turned Vegetables shaped into neat barrel shapes using a small paring knife.

Specialist suppliers

As we have all our supplies delivered direct to the restaurant, buying is quite easy. But we are still a hostage to availability, the weather and seasonal quality. If a certain foodstuff is not up to standard then we do without rather than put on a sub-standard dish. Here is a list of some of my local suppliers plus a few other useful food shops and chef's equipment suppliers, several of whom provide a mail-order service.

First, let me recommend *Henrietta Green's Food Lovers' Guide to Britain*, 1996–97 (BBC Books, £12.99) for a comprehensive, nationwide list of quality producers.

FISH
My fishmonger:
Colchester Oyster Fishery Ltd
Pyefleet Quay
Mersea Island
Colchester
Essex
CO5 8UN
Tel: 01206 384141
www.colchesteroysterfishery.com

Billingsgate Fish Market (*opens at 5.00 a.m. Tue–Sat*)
Trafalgar Way
Poplar
London
E14 5ST
Tel: 020 7987 1118

For a list of quality fishmongers in your area, contact:
The National Federation of Fishmongers
Pisces
London Road
Feering
Colchester
CO5 9ED
Tel: 01376 571391

MEAT
My butcher:
Billfields Food Co. Ltd
Unit 2 & 3
57 Sandygate Street
London
SE15 1LE
Tel: 0870 770 6920
www.billfields.co.uk

For a list of butchers who will supply not only excellent meat but also items such as foie gras, caul fat, oxtails etc., contact:

The Guild of Q Butchers
PO Box 26139
Dunfermline
Fife
KY12 7WJ
Tel: 01383 432622
www.guildofqbutchers.co.uk

FRUIT, VEGETABLES AND HERBS
My greengrocer:
Hyams and Cockerton
4-14 Southville
London
SW8 2PP
Tel: 020 7622 1167

Personal Catering Company
D1–D6 Fruit and Vegetable Market
New Covent Garden
London
SW8 5EE
Tel: 020 7498 4000

Wild Harvest (*mushrooms*)
31 London Stone Estate
Broughton
London
SW8 3QJ
Tel: 020 7498 5397

FINE FOOD STORES
Carluccio's (*mushrooms and oils*)
28a Neal Street
London
WC2H 9QT
Tel: 020 7240 1487
www.carluccios.com

The Food Market
Harvey Nichols & Co. Ltd
109-125 Knightsbridge
London
SW1X 7RJ
Tel: 0870 873 3833
www.harveynichols.com

Harrods Food Hall
87-135 Brompton Road
Knightsbridge
London
SW1X 7XL
Tel: 020 7730 1234
www.harrods.com

The Oil Merchant (*fine olive oils and truffle oils; mail-order*)
47 Ashchurch Grove
London
W12 9BU
Tel: 020 8740 1335

EQUIPMENT SUPPLIERS
Bamix of Switzerland (*mail-order*)
Unit 3, Ellesmere Business Park
Haydn Road
Sherwood
Nottingham
NG5 1DX
Tel: 0115 960 8646

Gilbert's Food Equipment (*catering suppliers; mail-order*)
Gilbert House
Borehamwood
WD6 1UA
Tel: 020 8731 3700

Lakeland Limited (*catering suppliers including Bake-O-Glide; mail-order*)
Alexandra Buildings
Windermere
Cumbria
LA23 1BQ
Tel: 015394 88100
www.lakelandlimited.com

Nisbet's (*catering suppliers; mail-order*)
1110 Aztec West
Bristol
BS32 4FA
Tel: 0845 1110281
www.nisbets.co.uk

Index

Acknowledgments

A book of this nature doesn't just happen within a few short weeks. It involves a host of different people working over many months, and I would like to express my gratitude to them.

First, I should like to thank my co-author, Roz Denny (aka Rose) who has been on call almost 24 hours a day. We shared a lot of laughter. My agents Fiona Lindsay and Linda Shanks, who together with Editorial Director Suzannah Gough and Editors Charlotte Coleman-Smith and Kate Bell, got the whole book off the ground. Geoff Lung flew over specially from Australia to interpret my style of food in the greatest way possible and created pictures that leave me breathless.

A good chef puts his trust in a strong team. I have a dedicated kitchen brigade and front of house staff who have helped to make the Aubergine the success it is. My team of cooks I hold in complete awe. Marcus Waring and Mark Askew were my two sous-chefs during the period offering not only advice with the book but also helping run the kitchen whilst I dealt with Roz's questions. Other cooks include Freddie Foster, chef de partie, whose bouncing enthusiasm is infectious; my pastry chef Damien Allsop, who displays admirable and inspiring skill; Angela Hartnell for her calm efficiency; and Ian Mappin for his valuable back-up support. In addition, the Aubergine would not have been but for the tireless support of my business associates (and good friends) Claudio Pulze, Guliano Lotto, Franco Zanellato, Lee Collier and Martin Pope.

My suppliers, too, have been more than generous with their produce and products for photography: Nick Greene of Villeroy and Boch ensured a never-ending stream of perfect china and plates; Tony Allen, Mark Allen and Ronnie Truss of Cutty Catering, Steven Bird of Cove Shellfish, Bournemouth, and Steve Downey of Heritage Fine Foods all brought in outstandingly fresh fish and top-quality foie gras; Butcher Toby Baxendale of Billfields delivered meat in its prime; Christian, Blair and Paul Cockerton of Hyams and Cockerton, Battersea, supplied wonderful fresh vegetables and fruits; Mike de Strumello of Wild Harvest provided fantastic fungi; and Richard Fordham installed my kitchen with Bonnet cookers.

Finally, to Tana, just simply: thank you.

The Publisher would like to thank the following: Tessa Clayton for editorial assistance, Penelope Cream for proofreading and Hilary Guy for providing the props for photography.